BIRMINGHAM AT WAR
1939–45

Your Towns & Cities in World War Two

BIRMINGHAM AT WAR
1939–45

JULIE PHILLIPS

Pen & Sword
MILITARY

First published in Great Britain in 2018 by
PEN & SWORD MILITARY
An imprint of
Pen & Sword Books Ltd
47 Church Street
Barnsley
South Yorkshire S70 2AS

ISBN 978 1 47386 697 3

A CIP catalogue record for this book is available from the British
Library.

Printed and bound in England
by CPI Group (UK) Ltd, Croydon, CR0 4YY

Typeset in Times New Roman by SRJ Info Jnana System Pvt Ltd.

Pen & Sword Books Limited incorporates the Imprints of
Atlas, Archaeology, Aviation, Discovery, Family History, Fiction,
History, Maritime, Military, Military Classics, Politics, Select,
Transport, True Crime, Air World, Frontline Publishing, Leo Cooper,
Remember When, Seaforth Publishing, The Praetorian Press,
Wharncliffe Local History, Wharncliffe Transport, Wharncliffe True
Crime and White Owl.

For a complete list of Pen & Sword titles please contact
PEN & SWORD BOOKS LIMITED
47 Church Street, Barnsley, South Yorkshire, S70 2AS, England
E-mail: enquiries@pen-and-sword.co.uk
Website: www.pen-and-sword.co.uk

Contents

Acknowledgements

I am indebted to, and full of gratitude and admiration for, so many people who generously gave their time, memories and experience in the making of this book:

Caroline Bagnall
Birmingham Air-Raids Remembrance Association (BARRA)
Birmingham Archives – the Wolfson Centre
Birmingham City Council
Birmingham City Council Film and Television Office
Birmingham Mail
Birmingham Memories/Facebook Group
Birmingham History and Other Stuff/Facebook Group
Birmingham in Photos, Now and Then/Facebook Group
Birmingham Post
Michael and Sheila Brightlee
Cadbury Archive, Mondelez International
David Edwards
Jacqui Fielding and family
Sarah Foden and Jackie Jones, Cadbury Archive, Mondelez International
Ann Hodgetts
Eileen Housman and family
Keith Iddes and family
London RAF Museum
Toby Neal
Bob Parish
Douglas and Eileen Perry and family
David Phillips
Victor de Quincey and family
The Royal Orthopaedic Hospital, Birmingham, NHS Trust Archive
Jackie Sayle and family
Radio Shropshire
Don Smith and family
Shropshire Star
Moira Taylor and family

Fran Tracey and family
Wartime Birmingham and the Blitz/Facebook Group
Lorna Webb and family

Every effort has been made to ensure that image captions and copyright/permissions are correct. If there are any errors or oversights, please contact the publisher so that they may be rectified.

Dedication

This book is dedicated to the many people who gave their time and memories for this book and to the brave and determined people of Birmingham who saw the city through the dark years of the Second World War and helped in its recovery.

Introduction

Barely seventeen years after the long and treacherous Great War of 1914–1918, Birmingham was once more being forced to take part in yet another world war. The Great War had been labelled the war to end all wars, with significant efforts upon the part of the League of Nations to prevent such a world crisis from ever happening again falling apart with the invasion of Poland by Germany in 1935.

It must have been a scene of *déjà vu*, with many in the city having not yet forgotten the horror and hardship that the First World War had cruelly bestowed upon them. Despite the recession and continuing hardship felt by Birmingham and many other towns and cities across the country, once more the people of Birmingham, from the ordinary working class to those in power and more affluent, were prepared to do what they could to help Britain triumph over Hitler. They were not going to merely stand by and let Germany trample over their freedom and way of life.

The contribution of Birmingham to the Second World War was vast, as was the damage it sustained through the battering of the Blitz. It is far beyond the scope of this book to highlight every single event, heroics and contribution that its citizens and community had to undertake to make the war a little easier for all concerned. This book, therefore, gives a snapshot of the period, examining the contribution of its workforce, its community and the powers that be.

CHAPTER ONE

A Brief History of Birmingham

Birmingham has always been a strategic and important place in the British Isles. It was first referred to in the *Domesday Book*, 1086, as a farming community, a poor relation to the more affluent areas of nearby King's Norton and Aston. The area started off relatively small with around 100 inhabitants. The origins of how the name Birmingham came to be is subject to some disagreement but Bermingeham, as it was spelled in the *Domesday Book,* is a combination of words from the Anglo-Saxon: Brem/Beorma (a person's name), ingas (meaning descendants) and ham (meaning home).

There is evidence of a settlement from around 3,000 years ago by way of burnt mounds that are believed to be where cooking took place, or possibly the sites of saunas. It wasn't until the Romans came in 43AD that the first main roads were built, along with a major fort near Edgbaston. Then came the German settlers.

The settlements remained small and it wasn't until 1166 when the king granted Peter de Birmingham, the lord of the manor, permission to hold a market that we see the tremendous growth of the city begin. What made it an excellent site for trade was the position of the River Rea and a suitable crossing. Traders first came from across the borders in Wales to sell their sheep and cattle.

It wasn't long before several local industries and trades developed. With the coming of the cattle a whole industry based on leather evolved. As transport and trade links were strengthened, Birmingham saw raw materials, such as iron and coal, brought in alongside clay for the potteries. The river was also invaluable in that it provided the resources for washing and dyeing cloth.

Birmingham was becoming a boomtown and by the 1300s it was the third largest town in the county of Warwickshire behind only Warwick and Coventry. From its lowly beginnings, its trade and industry had seen its inhabitants swell to around 1,000. Birmingham also had its own particular dialect, resulting in its people being affectionately known as Brummies – but woe betide the well-meaning tourist who mistakes other dialects from the Black Country or West Midlands as Brummie.

Unfortunately, this rapid period of growth and expansion was to come to a halt in the fourteenth century with the arrival of the plague – the Black Death. This devastating disease arrived aboard sailing ships from Genoa that docked in Sicily. Many of the ships' passengers and crew had mysteriously died, the only clues to their demise being the horrendous black boils that covered their bodies. The plague had come to Europe and it wasn't long until it invaded Britain. Over five years the Black Death killed an estimated one-third of Europe's population – that's a staggering 20 million people. Birmingham was not immune to the devastating effects of the plague and its population declined.

By the 1500s, Birmingham had managed to rally and saw a decent population increase to around 1,500. This rose again in the 1700s to around 8,000 inhabitants. The main industry of the period, metal work, including gun production, saw around 200 forges in the area in 1683, with everything from nails, brass candlesticks, ironwork and swords produced. It wouldn't be the last time that the city would see the manufacturing of guns and ammunition.

Its association with arms became more pronounced during the Civil War of 1642–1651. Due to tensions between Charles I and his allegiance to the church and the puritan-associated parliament, Birmingham saw attention drawn to their sword- and gun-making prowess with their supply to the parliamentary forces. If the people of Birmingham thought they would get away with such heresy, they were about to receive a rude awakening. The morning of Easter Monday 1643 dawned as usual until the unsuspecting inhabitants were confronted by a 2,000-strong army led by Prince Rupert, marching to teach them a lesson. Because Birmingham was not a fortified town, they met with little resistance and had free reign to attack the people and ransack their homes. There is still damage caused by this battle to be seen on the staircase of Aston Hall today.

Despite these troubles the population had grown again by the eighteenth century, up to 15,000, rendering it the fastest-developing town. By the nineteenth century, it had expanded again to almost 74,000, as people swept in to the area from across the country. It was fast becoming a metropolitan town with immigrants from

Council House, Birmingham. Author's own.

Africa and the West Indies alongside European Jewish refugees, a tradition that continues today.

There was no stopping the town, which saw its industrial heart grow and grow. One of its industries was brass and in the eighteenth century fittings were made for horses and carriages, buttons and buckles. With the price of metal rising and to lessen their reliance on exports those brass manufacturers were forced to rethink their strategies. This came via the formation of the Birmingham Metal Company, which was situated at the Brass House on Broad Street. Birmingham was put on the map as the centre for brass-making. To reduce costs in transport as the town's narrow and ineffective roads were damaged by the heavily laden carts, canals were constructed by engineer James Brindley, who built the canal from Birmingham to Wednesbury. Eventually this canal system would be expanded, joining the town to the Severn, Mersey, Trent and Thames, and to important ports such as Liverpool and Hull.

It wasn't just industry that was booming in the town. Education and free thinking was also blossoming with the grammar school and a group known as the Lunar Society. This was formed by men of the scientific, literary and business persuasion with inventors. They met in the town at Boulton House, Handsworth, whenever the moon was full, with the remit to make new discoveries and understanding of the natural world and medicine, build factories and make new machines, such as the steam engine, and make waves against slavery, amongst other things. Prominent members of the group included: Erasmus Darwin – doctor and writer; Josiah Wedgewood – industrialist; James Watt – inventor; and William Witherington – the doctor who was to discover the drug digitalis (digoxin) from the foxglove plant, used to treat heart problems. The society petered out in the 1800s, but they left a legacy for the modern world.

A chapter on the history of Birmingham would not be complete without mentioning its part in anti-slavery. As has been mentioned before, the town had a great gun-making industry, the products of which were sold in Africa to buy slaves on the sugar plantations. They also made slave chains. There were some in the local community who opposed this and they set up a campaign to abolish slavery. They had special badges made by Josiah Wedgewood with the slogan 'Am I not a man and a brother?' written on them. In 1806, the slave trade was abolished.

There were many trades in Birmingham, including leather-work, guns and pottery. This paved the way for many different areas of the town to be associated with certain trades. One of these was the Jewellery Quarter, a collection of small businesses.

The Art Gallery, Birmingham. Author's own.

One young jeweller's family, Jacob Jacobs from Sheffield, moved to Birmingham in 1852 and set up premises in Vittoria Street. Because of the lack of trade in the industry, as a ploy to garner more trade, much in the way that celebrities are used to endorse products today by advertisers, HRH Alexandra, the Princess of Wales, wore Birmingham jewellery.

In 1887, trade had picked up sufficiently for the introduction of the Birmingham Jewellers' and Silversmiths' Association, which founded a school for workers. There were once over 30,000 people working there and part of that era still stands today with museums and workshops.

Birmingham had and still has many trades including glass (the windows in Crystal Palace originated from Birmingham), screws manufactured in Smethwick, Ansells Brewery and the Midland Vinegar factories, along with powdered custard and HP Sauce. One of the other big industries was pen-making, when Joseph Gillott came to Birmingham from Sheffield in 1822, where he had previously made knives and other small metal items. His endeavour was so successful that he expanded the business in 1839.

The Town Hall, Birmingham. Author's Own.

With the growth in industry there had to be somewhere to house all the workers. An unfortunate by-product of the success in industry was that this led to more pollution and overcrowding. Something had to be done and fast. A special board (the Birmingham Street Commissioners) was set up in 1769 that would help to clean up the streets and bring some order.

We then began to see real change in the streets and structure of Birmingham. People were concerned about crime and the fact there was very little by way of order and governance. One prominent man involved in this was Joseph Chamberlain, who was Mayor of Birmingham from 1873–1876. His vision was revolutionary and his changes paved the way for Birmingham to become the great city it is today. He was dismayed by the lack of education for workers' children and was also keen to modernise the voting system. He became MP for Birmingham under the Liberal party and was involved in founding the University of Birmingham.

In 1838, the first council was formed and in 1851 took responsibility of the work started by the Street Commissioners. This involved the sanitation of the water supply and setting the rails for the trams. By 1901, Birmingham's population had risen to over 522,200 and the town was given city status by Queen Victoria in 1889. It's true that people in Birmingham can drink water from Wales due to the determination of Chamberlain to improve Birmingham's lot. They started to build a reservoir in 1894 in the Elan valley to the tune of £6.6 million (£778,800,000 at today's values). It was opened in 1904 by King Edward VII.

During the First World War, many of the local trades and industries turned their attention to war-work, including women working in munitions factories. Austin Motors in the city at Longbridge manufactured motor cars, producing 1,500 vehicles a year and employing 2,000 workers by the start of the Second World War. When the Second World War began, they diversified to help the war effort by producing aircraft, guns and trucks.

Another prominent concern in Birmingham was that of the Quaker Cadbury family. They built a factory in Bournville in 1878, manufacturing chocolate and cocoa. Just as Chamberlain had, George Cadbury was interested in the health of the population, particularly those who worked for the family, so he decided to

Corporation Street, Birmingham. Author's Own.

build decent homes to get them out of their squalid, back-to-back houses.

The Bournville Village Trust was founded in 1900 and was granted permission to have more land for houses. The village included sports facilities, parks, a local school and shops. The

New developments, Birmingham, 2016. Author's Own.

village was heralded as gold standard and people visited from across the globe.

At the end of the First World War the world suffered a financial slump. The war had affected everyone deeply, no less the appalling loss of life – Birmingham itself had seen 148,000 of its men enlist, 11,000 of whom were never to return. Unemployment was rife and Britain was on her knees. Things for Birmingham, however, were perhaps more favourable than elsewhere. It would be less than twenty years later that the call of war would sound again and Birmingham was to have one of its worst periods in history.

Today, Birmingham is a vibrant, multicultural, modern city with around 1.1 million people living and working there. The city goes against the trend where in the rest of the UK there is an older population – most in the city are young, aged 20–24, probably due to the popularity of the university. Despite the battering it took in the Second World War and the closure of many factories between the 1970s–1990s, it has expanded again and regeneration is taking place all the time. So, what did happen to Birmingham in the Second World War? How did they cope and what was their contribution to the war effort?

Library and Baskerville House in Centenary Square, Birmingham, 2016.
Author's Own.

CHAPTER TWO

War Breaks Out

Birmingham did its utmost to support the war effort in the Great War and the people of Birmingham were quite rightly relieved when it was all over. The Great War had been titled the war to end all wars but, despite the formation of the League of Nations and negotiations to prevent such a bloody and costly war from happening again, tensions prevailed and less than twenty years after the end of the First World War, it looked as though the world was about to find itself embroiled in yet another conflict.

It took a long time for Britain to recover from the Great War. In the immediate aftermath came a recession. Not only had people suffered great losses of their menfolk on the battlefields and seas of the conflict, supplies were still scarce and the make-do-and-mend mentality had to continue for years after the war ended. Jobs were scarce and many women who had found themselves employed at the plough and in the factories suddenly had to return to the home as the men that survived and returned took back what jobs there were. The last thing they needed was another long, drawn-out conflict.

But why did the Second World War start and why was Britain compelled, as it had been in the Great War, to intervene? Germany was financially ruined because of the First World War. There was high unemployment with the then government coming under fire. This gave the National Socialist Party (Nazis), headed by Adolf Hitler, the right environment to launch their campaign. Hitler had fought in the Great War and took the defeat badly, seeking revenge. But to achieve his goal he needed to gain support and power first.

He was granted his wish when the National Socialist Party won the election in 1932 and he became Chancellor of Germany.

In 1934, he became führer. His campaign had been built on selling the German people a dream of improved infrastructure with more emphasis placed on manufacturing. This came at a price, however, as he also began to interfere in his people's freedom and liberty, including the persecution of Jews.

Britain was intrinsically involved at this stage, having been at the forefront of chastisement for Germany for the destruction they had previously wreaked on the rest of the world. In 1935, Germany and Britain signed a treaty that would permit Germany to increase the size of its naval fleet. The Treaty of Versailles that was drawn up as part of the peace process following the Great War was a thorn in Hitler's side and he was determined to have it revoked. He was also unhappy with some of the treaty's terms, particularly that Germany, amongst other sanctions, was still having to pay compensation to the countries it invaded and had lost some of its land.

On the quiet, Germany was strengthening its forces again with pilots training in gliders as they were not allowed an air force. Hitler meant serious business and this was shown when his army retook the Rhineland. Whilst this was happening, other countries were also rebuilding their armed forces. Britain had initially underestimated the threat from Germany and the size of its army before the Great War and had consequently been woefully unprepared. They were not going to make that mistake again. Old rivalries and old scores that had remained unsettled since the Great War were beginning to boil to the surface again. The League of Nations, set up to keep the peace and help to prevent anything as heinous as the Great War from ever happening again, was unable to stop it. The war machine had, once again, been set in motion.

Britain was drawn into war when Germany invaded Poland in 1939. Hitler, the leader, had been gaining popularity and building his army. The then prime minister of Great Britain, Neville Chamberlain, declared war on Germany on 3 September 1939.

Adolf Hitler joined the Bavarian Army at the age of 25, at the commencement of the Great War. Having been injured in that conflict, he became involved in the much-depleted German Army as an intelligence officer, attempting to infiltrate the German Workers' Party, his focus increasingly becoming anti-Semitic. He decided that the world needed ridding of Jews, blaming them for

Germany's problems. Under his auspices, the party became the National Socialist German Workers party, adopting the swastika as their emblem. Deploring the Treaty of Versailles, he publicly denounced it, raging against what he saw as the unfair treatment and sanctions doled out to the German people. Due to the instability of several states surrounding Germany, Hitler took the opportunity to use this to his advantage.

There were several events after the Great War that enabled Hitler to push closer and to revisit unfinished business and settle old scores. The first of these was the Spanish Civil War, followed closely by the annexation of Austria, the invasion of Czechoslovakia and the occupation of the Sudetenland. All conspired to give Germany the strength and opportunity to invade Poland. Hitler did not see Great Britain as a threat, believing it to suffer from weak leadership. He was convinced that his strategic positioning and methods of warfare would reign supreme and that there was no other power on Earth that could stop his takeover bid. The Second World War had started and preparations were gathering pace all over the country.

One such preparation was the rota for the calling-up of men. Those already in the regular forces were called back to their units, but there was to be a phased calling-up of volunteers. In January 1940, men who were aged 20 and above but would not be 23 on 1 December 1940 were called-up. The first wave had already been sent their papers and were expected to report to their training units. Nationally, there were 250,000 men in this group and they had been registered on 9 December 1939.

The time to complete registration and all the calling-up documentation and checks was expected to take up to three months in most cases. There were guidelines as to the order in which men would be called-up, priority being given to those who could more easily be spared from their occupations and the needs of the particular units they were to go to. The next set of registrations for class 20 to 24 was due to start in February 1940.

Consideration was also being given to those in class 20 to 28, who it was thought should be able to go on active service, whereas those men in class 35 to 42 were expected to stay in home defence. This then left the men in class 28 to 35 to be allocated to either service at home or abroad.

RCS Royal Corps of Signals, 48 City of Birmingham Squadron.
The reverse of this image is handwritten: Our gang. 48 Squad. Oct 10th,
1938 – Feb 4th 1939. Author's Own.

It had been recognised that industry would struggle greatly should the demand grow for more men to be called-up. It was therefore hoped that each successive group would be smaller than the one preceding it, to help industry cope.

It was also unclear how many men would be needed as no one knew how long the war would go on for. Britain had been taught a lesson in the Great War, which had been expected to last only until Christmas 1914. It raged on for four years. They knew not to underestimate the enemy and were determined to enter this war better prepared.

CHAPTER THREE

Evacuation

For the most part, in the early months of the war, life in Birmingham and the rest of Great Britain carried on as usual. Despite the huge upheaval involving servicemen being called-up, everyday life remained the same. Things were about to change, with the German *Luftwaffe* bombing major cities and ports.

While the upheaval was going on, the British Government were left with a problem: how could they protect the British public from being bombarded night after night? In short, they were limited to what they could do. They had little intelligence as to how long these raids would go on for and often little warning that they were coming. The British public, despite all the precautions that were put in place, were sitting ducks.

This was until Operation *Pied Piper* was implemented on 1 September 1939. British children who lived in the areas most at risk from bombing were evacuated out to safer areas of the country. Many were sent to Wales, Cornwall, Devon and East Anglia, with some being sent to Canada, Australia and the USA. And although efforts were made to keep siblings together, it wasn't always possible.

One can only imagine what it was like as a young child to be sent away from everything they knew and the people they loved, not knowing if they would see them again. Many did return home but found they had changed, and with the impact on their lives with parents and children not seeing each other for months, sometimes years, many found it difficult to adjust on their return. However, many also remained in touch with their hosts and became part of these new extended families.

This was happening up and down the county and in Birmingham, because towns were a target due to the factories manufacturing items such as ammunition and aeroplanes. It was inevitable that evacuation would take place on a great scale.

The *Birmingham Post*, in its pages of the 18 November 1939 issue, told of a scheme that was coming into force, organised by the Minister of Transport, to make it easier for parents of evacuated children to visit their offspring. This would involve reduced rail fares, but the newspaper made it clear that this was very much a pilot scheme with authorities 'working in the dark'. Special vouchers would be issued to parents via the schools.

It was hoped that arrangements could be made to prevent families from having to walk some distance from railway stations to where their children were, with the possibility of pick-up points near to the stations families could be transported from, or their children being brought there. The Ministry Offices in Birmingham were keen to help those parents who lived in other key regions in the country, such as Manchester and Liverpool, whose children were billeted in Warwickshire.

The other issue was that of compulsory attendance at school. With so many children away from the city and the constant threat of bombing, not forgetting the need for some children to work, particularly in agricultural work, some schools in the worst affected areas of Birmingham had been closed or commandeered as First Aid posts or for storage of items such as gas-masks.

The assistant education officer, R.E. Cousens, was keen to ensure schools were re-opened and that this should happen in the 'neutral' zones of the city (areas of the city less likely to be bombed). There would be sufficient protective measures taken for around 10,000 schoolchildren in Birmingham, and compulsory attendance would resume as soon as these measures, which included shelters, had had the necessary inspections and were deemed appropriate.

Because the threat of bombing was still apparent, those schools operating as decontamination centres and First Aid posts would be required to share buildings in shifts, so that children could continue their schooling.

Another scheme was via Greenmore College, 37–40 Union Street, Birmingham. They were concerned about the education of children who had not been evacuated and so offered courses for them. There was preparatory training for girls and boys aged 8 and over, as well as a higher education certificate, business and secretarial courses and preparation for civil service exams.

Short courses in wireless operation in the Merchant Navy was another government-initiated scheme for those aged 16 and over. They would train at the Wireless College in Sefton Park Road, Liverpool, and this would be a reserved occupation.

But the bombing didn't just affect the children. Teachers found themselves in hardship because they could not work in schools that had been temporarily closed. Many of these teachers accompanied their classes out of Birmingham when they were evacuated and worked by keeping an eye on the children in their new homes as well as teaching them. Many of those who stayed behind offered their services as volunteers in the various First Aid and other organisations to help the war effort. There was also another scheme for relief of the 800 teachers from Birmingham who worked in those zones of the city that had been evacuated. They could opt to take part in an exchange of duties for a term, working in other areas and disciplines in the city.

Not all children were evacuated immediately and some never were, their parents preferring to keep them close. David Edwards was a young child living in Birmingham when war broke out. He remembers the Anderson shelter at the bottom of his garden and recalls having to rush down there with his family at night. The family had two shelters, one at the bottom of the garden and another one under the stairs. One night there was a huge blast that destroyed houses just six doors down from his. He said this was the overriding memory for him of the Blitz. Terrifying as this was, as children they soon found lighter moments and used the bomb damage as their playground. He remembers sailing his tin bath in a big bomb crater that had filled with water.

His family were involved in the war effort. His sister was a lorry driver, delivering ammunition and war equipment, such as rifles and revolvers for BSA, who had a factory in the city.

He was eventually evacuated out near Kidderminster and was only a few miles away from his brother. His host family had a daughter and the local school had arranged houses for evacuees.

Another evacuee, Bob Parish, who was born in 1932 and lived in Arthur Street, not far from the BSA factory in Small Heath, was evacuated in 1942. Before he left he witnessed many of the bombing raids on the city. He can remember, when the sirens went at night, being grabbed by his parents and taken to the house down the road. He could see Small Heath from their attic. He remembers the time the BSA factory was badly hit. A bomb hit the first floor of the four-storey building, making it collapse, the falling building and machinery inside killing around eighty workers.

Birmingham experienced a lot of poverty and Bob's family was just one of many who lived in the slum areas, with back-to-back housing, outdoor shared privies and not a lot of money coming in. Their family, like many others in the city, were no strangers to hardship and tragedy. Bob was adopted by his aunt when he was 2 after his mother died in an accident.

Not all evacuated children were sent to live with strangers. Some were lucky enough to have relatives living in the countryside and could go and live there for the duration of the war. Ann Hodgetts was one such child. She saw none of the bombing and destruction of the Blitz on Birmingham because she was evacuated to live with her aunt, a district nurse, and family in Chesterfield, Derbyshire, where there were a lot of other evacuees. She left behind her mother and father. Her father at the time was in the police force and worked through the war fire-watching in Digbeth. When the threat of invasion from German forces came, he was sent to Portsmouth. Although relatively safe in Chesterfield compared to Birmingham, Ann recalls hearing enemy planes flying overhead, and remembers looking over the edge of a bomb crater at nearby Ashover.

When the sirens went off it was Ann's job to grab the gas-masks that hung on the back door. The only way they really kept up with the news on the war was through listening to the wireless. One of the substantial changes that happened to her as a result of being evacuated was it changed her accent, because of the time she spent living and being schooled in Derbyshire.

Her change of circumstances enforced by war was happening to thousands of children up and down the country, but for her, as for many others in her situation, being evacuated had its advantages. Her brother Roger and she worked on a farm, helping to bring the sterilised milk home, which she much preferred to the milk they had in Birmingham. They made rosehip syrup, helped with the hay-making, and knitted socks for soldiers at war. There was plenty to occupy them and try to keep their minds off what was happening to their families in Birmingham. They were also visited several times by their grandparents, who lived in Sparkbrook, a reminder of home.

Some evacuees came and went between their homes and those of their host families several times. Eileen Housman was just 5 years old when the war broke out and was living in Aston, Birmingham. She was evacuated, aged 7, to friends of her grandparents living in Stourport-on-Severn. While she was there, her parents moved to Edgbaston and she acquired a new baby brother.

She remembers her parents coming on a Midland Red bus to visit her, bringing her baby brother with them. They'd all have lunch with the host family, with the baby lying in a wicker basket on a fold-up table that sat underneath the main table. She can recall the white sticky tape on the windows. This was put on to prevent the glass shattering should a bomb-blast occur nearby.

While they were drinking their tea, her mother commented that she could hear a German plane approaching. The mother of the host family said they didn't get German planes flying over and that it must be a friendly British plane. Her mother was adamant, and her instincts turned out to be correct. After a few minutes, they heard a terrific bang followed by another one – they were German bombs. The bomb had hit the school at the end of the road and another had detonated in someone's back garden. Her mother bundled her out of the house exclaiming, 'If you can get bombed here, you can get bombed anywhere. You're coming home with us.'

Her father worked in the sheet metal industry at the Austin factory. This was a reserved

Douglas and Eileen Perry (now Housman). Courtesy of Eileen Housman.

occupation at the time and they lived in a tiny back-to-back house with a living room, pantry, one bedroom and one other room. They were unable to use the attic room because a landmine had gone over and taken part of the roof with it.

Because the bombing was worse in Birmingham, she was evacuated again to her mum's friends' house, who were Quakers and lived near Tenbury Wells. The family already had a boy of their own who was aged 7 – she was 10. They lived in a black-and-white cottage and she called them Aunty Phyl and Uncle Harry. She also attended the local school there. Because Aunty Phyl was expecting a baby, Eileen was moved to another family nearby with a mum, dad, a girl her age, two boys and a grandad. They also housed another evacuee, John Owens, but his mum took him home soon after.

Eileen eventually went home at Christmas 1943, because something had upset her mother and she demanded that she go home with her. She remembers hearing and seeing quite a few bombs dropped on the city, particularly onto the factories and nearby St Thomas's Church. But despite the separation from her family and the danger from the bombs, the family survived and in March 1944 her baby sister was born.

She recalls life in Birmingham. Her grandparents at one point lived in Barton Street, Aston, near to the Barton Arms, which is still in business today. Birmingham Hippodrome was just around the corner and the trams passed nearby. Her grandmother was the local midwife and she also assisted the local doctor and helped when people died. Her grandfather was a caster in Birmingham. Their neighbours had a boy who would become one of Birmingham's mayors. Her father, William Perry, was in the ARP for his section.

Being evacuated had a long-lasting effect on Eileen as she kept in touch with Phyl and Harry after the war, going back for holidays and eventually becoming godmother to one of their daughters. The whole family treated her as an older sister and not an evacuee. In fact, being an evacuee meant that she went back to the farm and met a farmhand who was to become her husband. They are still married sixty years later.

Another couple, who were to marry after the war, didn't live far away from each other in Birmingham. Michael Brightlee was born in Edgbaston and his wife Sheila was born in Harborne.

Michael's father worked in the Jewellery Quarter and at age 10, Michael wrote out the invoices for him, often on the back of cigarette packet card to save paper. There was a paper shortage during the war and people were encouraged to re-use paper and reduce use wherever possible. Sheila's father was a manager at George Mason's, a grocer's shop in Birmingham.

Michael witnessed the heavy bombing of his area. There were semi-detached houses on Wadhurst Road, just off City Road, and when war came they had a 'safe' place under the stairs and their father helped with the fire-watching, while both his brothers were away in the army. When the sirens sounded, he'd sit under the stairs with his mother, playing a game, and he'd sleep under the large, heavy, old oak dining room table with his head under the sideboard.

One night a flying bomb came down across the gardens towards City Road and exploded, blowing in the back of the house. His parents tore down the stairs, fearing the worst. There was no noise coming from the dining room because Michael had slept through the whole commotion.

Sheila remembers the rationing of sweets and having coupons to spend. Her father was a grocer and when sugar was rationed they had to give it up. She remembers the powdered eggs and Spam. She also remembers the bombing, particularly an incendiary bomb that missed their house but hit concrete, failing to detonate but burning a hole in it. They had an Anderson shelter in their back garden, which had a lawn laid over the top of it. As a child, she used to go shrapnel-hunting with her friends.

At school, they were subjected to air-raid shelter and gas-mask drills. They had identity bracelets and necklaces, as this was often the only way bodies involved in blasts could be identified. She also recalls that the local buses were not kept in the depot at night for fear of a bomb strike, so they were parked on the roadside. She remembers cheekily giving their bells a ding on the way to school. Neither of them as children felt the fear of bombing raids and state that it was down to the attitude and example of the parents. It was very much a case of keep calm and carry on.

The whole family was involved in the war effort by fire-watching, fighting in the army and working in the Auxiliary Territorial Service (ATS). Formed in 1938, the ATS was an amalgamation of three key services: the emergency services; First Aid Nursing Yeomanry; and the Women's Legion. Its primary role was to support the armed forces with activities such as driving duties and secretarial work. It was never combatant. By 1940, the service had around 34,000 members. One of its most famous members was Princess Elizabeth, who joined in 1944, following improvements and expansion to the service that had come under the jurisdiction of military law in 1941 and became better regulated with higher standards of accommodation and status. Even at home, Sheila's family saw nothing went to waste and they turned their garden over to grow vegetables in the Dig for Victory campaign.

The war effort was very much a family affair in most cases in Birmingham and across the country. Sons, fathers, brothers and uncles were often away fighting, or undertaking war-work in the city and further afield, while mothers, sisters, aunts and daughters were in the munitions factories or the voluntary services doing their bit. They were at the plough and helping to get the harvest in, keeping the country going. Everyone had a part to play.

Don Smith was born in 1933, and as the country readied itself for impending war in 1939, he was in Selly Oak Hospital in Birmingham with suspected tuberculosis. The hospitals had been ordered to discharge non-serious cases to make way for the potential military and civilian casualties. He was transferred to the Bromwich Isolation Hospital, where he gained the attention of the local air-raid warden. The warden said that someone was sending Morse Code signals from the hospital at night. The resulting investigation showed that it was the light from Don's toy fire engine that his parents had given him for Christmas that was the source of the light and not a German spy. The matron took the batteries out.

In 1941, with the Blitz escalating, he was evacuated, as were many of his friends. He was sent to Guarlford in Worcestershire, and had a wonderful time there. His carers owned a pub, the Plough and Harrow, and the move from the industry and busyness of the city to the quiet rural area came as a bit of a shock to Don.

There was no electricity, running water or a flushing toilet. Instead there were oil lamps, a log-fired cooking range, a hand-operated pump for the water, and an earth toilet. His parents, however, missed him and were worried he was becoming too close to his carers and was moving away from them, so within eighteen months, they told him his carer was ill and could no longer look after him and moved him back to Birmingham with them.

The children evacuated from Birmingham were visited by their families in the communities they had been evacuated to, but they also came back to the city for breaks to be with their families. Christmas 1939 saw one such visit by elementary schoolchildren. The authorities had had concerns that the children and their families would find it difficult to be parted again when it was time to go back and that the evacuation scheme, as a result, would be put in jeopardy. Parents were warned to be careful. But, in reality, it all went well. According to the report, the majority of the 9,000 elementary children were, after Christmas, returned back to the safety zones.

Evacuation was a necessary but difficult event for the children of Birmingham. It undoubtedly saved and changed the lives of so many families forever.

CHAPTER FOUR

Terror from the Skies

It was soon becoming apparent to those fighting in and strategically planning it that the Second World War was going to be a very different beast to the one that raged less than twenty years earlier. For a start, there had been advances in artillery and the mechanics of war, but there was also the point that Germany had been defeated once and was not about to let that happen again.

In the early months the action had taken place pretty much off-stage and became known as the phoney war, because despite all the government and military warnings of the destruction and terrible things that were about to be unleashed, as far as the British public were concerned and had witnessed, life was going on pretty much as usual and they were warned against being lulled into a false sense of security. This was soon to change. From June 1940, the *Luftwaffe* began their assault across the skies, unleashing the Blitz. The RAF responded and the Battle of Britain was fought. Advances in warfare had seen the development of better bombs with more efficient and effective propulsion and guidance systems and a bigger, more destructive payload.

In Birmingham, the battle of the skies was to take place both on land and in the air. Birmingham was a key place for the building of aircraft and parts, which also made it a target for the *Luftwaffe*. Birmingham itself had many factories that were adapted during the Second World War to help with the war effort. Factories included Longbridge and the car manufacturer Austin Martin as well as the BSA company, producing bicycles. Many of these companies turned their hands to making planes, parts for planes, ammunition and army vehicles and parts, to name but a few to help with the war effort.

The *Blitzkrieg*, more popularly known as the Blitz, was the German term for lightning war. Its initial aim was to damage and force the enemy's armed forces into disarray with the use of specific and relentless targeting and firing of artillery. The first instance of this strategic way of fighting was in Poland in 1939, when the German forces decided to experiment. When this was deemed a successful campaign they rolled it out to Belgium, France and the Netherlands in the following year.

It wasn't long before British cities including London, Coventry and Birmingham were to feel the full force of this style of campaign. Birmingham had watched other cities being battered by bombs and practically razed to the ground. The people of Birmingham must have wondered when it was going to be their turn.

So why was Birmingham targeted? The first air-raid that Birmingham was to experience happened in August 1940. It became clear that German intelligence had been performing covert reconnaissance across British skies before the war started and they were only too aware of the layout of Birmingham and where the important factories and structures, such as gas works, hospitals, canals, telegraph and electricity facilities, were. This gave the Germans a huge advantage.

Birmingham was Britain's industrial workhorse. It was noted for its metal works, car manufacturing and the production of tools, including guns. The main industrial areas of the city that were of greatest concern were those with the greatest concentration of industrial units: Acocks Green, Castle Bromwich – where the airfield and factory were – Nechells, Wilton, Tyseley and Sparkbrook. It wasn't just the larger factories that were under threat, smaller industries were too. Birmingham also had a well-respected jewellery trade in the Jewellery Quarter, which became a potential target due to its work in producing small parts for guns.

One of the main reasons for being a target was the growing aerodrome and the development and manufacture of aircraft and parts. This was the thorn in Hitler's side. If Britain was capable of designing, developing, testing and manufacturing superior quality, efficient aircraft – better than that of Germany's – it would put a stick in the spokes of the wheel of Germany's campaign. The industry of Birmingham was a direct threat to Germany's success and the *Luftwaffe* couldn't allow that.

The *Luftwaffe*, or the German Air Force, was the biggest and most successful air force in Europe by the beginning of the Second World War. In Britain, the RAF itself had seen expansion and reform in the 1930s. Part of this expansion saw Austin take a factory near to its original Longbridge factory. This new factory was situated at Cofton Hackett, approximately 10 miles from the centre of Birmingham, near Bromsgrove.

Another example of Birmingham being at the forefront of the modernisation of the RAF was the fact that another factory, Morris Motors, led by Lord Nuffield, started producing Spitfires at Castle Bromwich. Rover, another company, was also was on the case, manufacturing aeroplane engines, first at Tyseley and then later at Solihull.

Taking a closer look at the new Austin factory, it was built in 1936 and they manufactured Fairey Battle aircraft and parts for the Bristol Mercury engines. It also built Gloster Gladiators and the Bristol Blenheim. The Bristol Blenheim was a light bomber that first took to the skies in 1935. It was one of the first all-metal, stressed-skin constructed craft with a powered gun turret. The Gloster Gladiator was a biplane fighter that first flew in 1934. The first Mercury engine was built in this factory in 1938, which led to hundreds of the Fairey Battles being constructed here, a cumbersome, when compared to other aircraft, single-engine light-bomber that was first flown in 1936.

The output and contribution to the war effort of just this one factory was phenomenal and one of many such factories across the city. Austin manufactured over 1,200 Fairey Battles, 330 Avro Lancasters, 300 Hawker Hurricanes and 3,000 Bristol Beaufighters, including wings and centre-pieces of other aircraft, alongside gun turrets, propellers and fuel tanks. Aircraft assembly was completed at Marston Green from 1941. Elmdon Aerodrome was where aircraft testing took place. The aircraft used to get towed across the London Midland and Scottish Railway to the airfield.

Looking now at Acocks Green, Rover took on a factory there in 1936 where they made parts for the Bristol Hercules engine. They also built gas turbine jet engines, but due to attention from the *Luftwaffe*, that work was shifted to Lancashire in 1941.

By far the biggest factory was at Castle Bromwich near the aerodrome. This was run by Nuffield and manufactured Spitfires with an initial order for 1,000. The factory cost £4 million (£239,789,076) to build, with the first Spitfire leaving the production line in June 1940. The Spitfire was the most produced and superior fighter and played a big part in securing victory for Britain.

One of the many families that experienced first-hand terror from the skies were the Quinceys. There had been heavy bombing raids throughout the city but one particular night in September 1940 saw the BSA factory in Small Heath targeted. The Quincey family lived right by this factory. The morning after the raid a terrified woman, who was pregnant, was taken by Victor Quincey down the railway embankment, which was still on fire from the bombing raid the night before, helped by her 4-year-old daughter and 11-year-old sister-in-law. They were eventually able to get on a train and flee to Ruabon in Wales, where she had the baby.

Victor de Quincey and mother May Quincey, 1940. Courtesy of Victor de Quincey.

The family returned to Birmingham in October after the baby was born only to find themselves in the middle of some of the most ferocious and destructive raids Birmingham had seen. In November, the BSA factory again was bombed, causing much damage and loss of life. The family's house was badly damaged, where they hid under the stairs. Three members of the family worked at the BSA factory.

While the family was suffering on the Home Front, Victor's uncle attempted to join-up at the tender age of 16, but his mother found out and stopped him. Eventually, his uncle, when he turned 17, did join-up with his brother, Victor's father, in June 1941. They had both wanted to join the navy, but by some mishap Victor's

Victor de Quincey and sister Jeanne Quincey, 1943. Courtesy of Victor de Quincey.

uncle joined the wrong queue and ended up with the Dorset Regiment.

Victor's father did join the navy and worked on Atlantic convoys at the White House in Washington, USA, for two years. After one crossing of the Atlantic aboard HMS *Rajah*, carrying home aircraft, he came back to Great Britain and joined a radar ship HMS *Boxer*, which took him to Ceylon. He wasn't demobilised until 1946 and, because he had volunteered, his job had not been kept open for his return.

Victor's uncle, in the meantime, was one of the first soldiers to land in Normandy in 1944 and two weeks after his 21st birthday was shot and badly wounded, but two Canadian soldiers helped him and he survived. He died in 2016 aged 93.

Victor and his sister were eventually evacuated to Wootton Wawen, 20 miles away from Birmingham, near Henley-in-Arden and Stratford-upon-Avon, but returned home after a couple of months.

Raymond Quincey. Dorset Regiment. Courtesy of Victor de Quincey.

Living near to these factories was a danger in itself, but it wasn't just those who lived nearby who were at risk. Those who worked in the factories or in the aerodromes themselves were also in peril, and not just from falling bombs.

One such man was Captain Neville Stacks who was chief test pilot at the Austin factory, Longbridge. Captain Stacks had enjoyed an illustrious flying career. Having served during the Great War, serving in France and Iraq, he retired from the RAF in 1919 but rejoined in 1921. Within five years he had earned the rank of captain, and with a competitive nature and desire to test the limits of any aeroplane and fly further than anyone else, he attempted to fly to India. According to reports, he was a 'daring' and 'skilful' pilot and loved aerobatic stunts. He

Victor Quincey's White House pass. Courtesy of Victor de Quincey.

even raced. In the 1929 King's Cup Race around England, he was one of forty-one planes that made it through the first stage, but he was forced to land during the final with just 30 miles to go.

Unperturbed, in 1931 he attempted England to Australia, but this was also hounded by bad luck and, although he managed to get to Vienna in the amazingly quick time for the age (seven hours), and then onto Constantinople in the same day, he had to return to England before he could complete his risky and daunting flight because of engine problems. He did try again twice, and again to India, but it wasn't to be.

On his return from Turkey, where he had been assisting the Turkish with handling the new planes he had delivered, he was appointed as chief test pilot to the Austin Aircraft Works. He was also chief instructor for the National Flying Services and, in 1935, was appointed air superintendent to Hilman's Airways.

On Tuesday 25 July 1939 at 7pm, whilst testing a plane with his mechanic, Harold Crawford, he crashed near the edge of the factory grounds. Both men were badly injured and taken to Selly Oak Hospital. Captain Stacks, who was from Middleton Hall Road, sustained two broken legs and suffered from shock, and Harold, from Bromsgrove, suffered a broken arm and cuts to his scalp.

This wasn't the only plane to crash in the area. On 20 February 1942, a Blenheim Z5899 plane hit a barrage balloon at Bearwood. Witnesses reported hearing the plane flying low and thought the pilot was looking for open ground to land on, but it crashed near Park Road and Warley Woods. It was piloted by Sergeant W.T. Kyle with Sergeant L.S. de Lisser and Sergeant E. Scott on board. They did not survive.

At the inquest in Smethwick, borough coroner Sydney Vernon recorded a verdict of accidental death. One witness, Fred Turner, who lived on the other side of the road from where the plane crashed, stated he had been in his garden when he saw the plane heading towards him. One of the houses, number 14 Park Road, where Mr and Mrs Rollason lived, was burned as a result of the crash, but they were at work at the time.

Another test pilot was Alex Henshaw, who was born in Peterborough and had some of his schooling in Stratford-upon-Avon. He soon became interested in motorcycles, which led to an interest in flying, resulting in his learning to fly at the Skegness East Lincolnshire Aero Club in 1932. His father had bought him a de Havilland Gipsy Moth, and he obtained his private pilot's licence on 6 June 1932.

Throughout the 1930s he became well-known and respected in air racing and air acrobatics. He won the Siddeley Trophy, the London to Isle of Man Race in 1937, and then the King's Cup in 1938. He then turned his attention to long-distance flying. On one of his epic and revolutionary journeys, on 5 February 1939, he flew from Gravesend to Cape Town, resting in Cape Town for twenty-eight hours before returning on 9 February, exhausted. The 12,754-mile round-trip took him an incredible four days, ten hours and sixteen minutes.

Following this, instead of joining the RAF he became the chief test pilot for Vickers Armstrong in Birmingham. So that he could fly in combat to protect the factory, he became a sergeant pilot, but the occasion never arose. He moved to Castle Bromwich, where he led a team of twenty-five. The testing of new aircraft straight off the factory floor was necessary but dangerous work. He lost two of his team through the process and had a few near misses himself, having endured many forced landings and one particular incident on 18 July 1942, when he crashed the plane he was testing between two houses in Wednesfield, near Wolverhampton. He also flew a plane down Broad Street, much to the surprise and delight of the crowds. The local police, however, were not impressed. Despite having a reputation as a dare-devil, he was awarded the MBE for his war service and lived into his 90s.

The city endured night after night of threat and bombardment from the skies, and it was down to the skill of the plane designers, builders and test pilots at the aerodromes and factories that played a big part in winning the war and protecting the inhabitants of Birmingham and wider afield. Without their expertise, bravery and determination, the outcome could have been very different.

CHAPTER FIVE

The Blitz and the Role of the ARP

Birmingham was under a siege from which there was very little protection. To begin with, the government could do nothing to stop the bombing raids, so Birmingham and many cities and towns had no choice but to hunker down and ride the raids out at great risk to residents' lives.

One of the first lines of defence came from the use of barrage balloons, which forced the enemy aircraft to fly at higher altitudes or risk being taken down by the balloons' steel cables. The RAF Balloon Command was formed, which had balloon centres across the country. Each centre was responsible for supplying and maintaining the balloons. Early on in 1939, the recruitment drive was on for Auxiliary Air Force Barrage Balloon squadrons, which would help defend Coventry and Birmingham. They wanted volunteers between the ages of 25 and 50, who would train through the summer months in the evenings and at weekends.

Birmingham had two regions in this set-up: the southern, which had two squadrons; and the northern, with three squadrons. Both were commanded via HQ in Birmingham. The areas including and between Oldbury and Elmdon (and the Castle Bromwich factory) were under the northern region, with the area around Solihull and Longbridge served by the southern region.

One of the squadrons from the northern region was sent to Boulogne, France, in February 1940, but when the enemy infiltrated the area they were evacuated to Calais and arrived back in Southampton in May the same year. By April 1940, four further squadrons were in France. It wasn't until the code words 'Aston Villa' were received by the RAF later that month that they were despatched to port, but they arrived back in RAF Cardington, Bedfordshire, a few weeks later.

Bennetts Hill. 11 April 1941. The Theatre Royal is at the bottom of the street. Note Beware Falling Debris sign and the pile of sandbags. Reproduced with the permission of the Library of Birmingham.

The balloons (168 of them) were flown in Birmingham from 10 May 1940. By now, there were four squadrons in Birmingham. West Bromwich had forty-eight balloons, Sutton Coldfield forty, Northfield forty, and Rowheath fifty balloons.

Barrage balloons were essentially a large bag (18.9 metres long and 7.6 metres in diameter) containing gas, which was anchored to the ground by a steel cable. They could be flown at varying altitudes up to a limit of 1,524 metres, and their aim was to force the enemy to fly higher, so preventing them from targeting accurately. They were filled with helium in the top section and allowed to fill up with air in the lower sections as they rose. The cables were also hazardous to unwitting pilots and more than capable of bringing aircraft down. The balloons would explode if shot and the falling cables caused injuries to personnel on the

Bishop Street. 16 October 1940. Note the ARP men and the policemen.
Reproduced with the permission of the Library of Birmingham.

ground. Their only Achilles heel were high winds and the risk of damage from shrapnel and bullets.

But the squadrons' task did not end with winching the balloons into position. They helped with civil defence duties both during and after the raids. They also tried to fool enemy aircraft by starting decoy fires in trenches that were dug and filled with petrol and ignited so that passing enemy planes would think it was a town on fire. These had the special codename of 'Starfish' sites. Examples of such sites in Birmingham included Balsall Common (14 miles to the south-east of Birmingham, near Solihull), Bickenhill (where Birmingham Airport is now situated) and Fairfield.

Although they had an important job to do during the Blitz campaign, only one enemy plane was brought down by the barrage balloons with two RAF planes suffering a similar fate.

The balloons were only a part of the defensive and wouldn't stop the more determined and skilled enemy pilot. What they needed was guns. Anti-aircraft artillery defence had been in the making since the early thirties. There was to be a 6-mile-deep

Lozells Picture House. 28 August 1942. Reproduced with the permission of the Library of Birmingham.

belt of guns to form an outer artillery zone alongside 20 miles of powerful searchlights. Those areas deemed important industrial areas, such as Birmingham, became gun-defended areas.

The Anti-Aircraft Command was formed on 1 April 1939 and came under the jurisdiction of RAF Fighter Command. It had seven divisions and the fourth of these looked after the Midlands and East Anglia. Birmingham had been allocated twenty-four 3.7-inch guns and sixteen 4.5-inch guns, which were heavy-calibre anti-aircraft guns, but not all were initially available. By the Blitz they had around seventy-one such guns under the command of 34 Brigade. By November 1940, there were twelve divisions and new boundaries were drawn with 11th Division being responsible for Birmingham and the West Midlands and Welsh Marches/North Wales, although by 1942, Birmingham and Coventry Divisions had joined together so the guns were not so widespread.

These guns were powerful. The bigger 4.5-inch gun was capable of shooting a 50-pound shell at least 40,000 feet in the air with the smaller 3.7-inch guns still packing a punch with a smaller shell but

Bristol Street. 27 October 1940. Brown Brothers Ltd – note soldier and women and man on his bicycle. Reproduced with the permission of the Library of Birmingham.

more rapid-fire rate. In 1941, Birmingham also had two reconditioned Great War guns at their disposable. These were light anti-aircraft guns, which were useful for warding off low-flying aircraft.

It is often said by those who survived the war that they could tell which plane was flying overhead, enemy or friendly. The German bombers had an easily recognisable noise to their engines, which were desynchronised to confuse the sound locators that were used to detect the aircraft.

Another form of defence developed at the time was that of the Observer Corps. It originated from the south and south-east of England in the Great War to monitor enemy aircraft movements. In 1938 the West Midlands had the Corps following the Munich Crisis – the argument over some of the Czechoslovakian border

Bull Ring, 10 April 1941. Hosing down buildings. Reproduced with the permission of the Library of Birmingham.

with Germany, known as the Sudetenland. Then in 1939, orders to mobilise were issued by the regional chief constables, and they began their monitoring, on which the air-raid ground-crews relied.

They operated in different areas and Birmingham was in Area 5. It had its HQ in Coventry but there were local posts at Selly Oak, Erdington and Shirley, amongst others. Area 5 was around 4,000 square miles in size. The operation was incredible. They tracked the flight paths of enemy aircraft across different areas. The route the German bombers took to get to the city of Birmingham was known as Heinkel Alley, via the Cotswolds.

Because the number of guns available fluctuated and were woefully inadequate against the onslaught of the *Luftwaffe*, Birmingham also had use of unrotated projectile rocket projectors, or Uncle Percy's, named after warfare expert Percy Hobart. They

Vine Avenue, Balsall Heath, off Runcorn Street. 18 September 1940. Note the white tape on the windows. Reproduced with the permission of the Library of Birmingham.

were relatively easy to make but there were problems and delays with training men to use them and in producing the projectiles themselves. One of the factories to use them in the city was the Austin factory, which had thirty-two of them. Some factories also had their outer walls painted in a camouflage pattern or to look like a row of houses in order to confuse the *Luftwaffe*.

Because more men were needed to go and fight, women from the ATS and, to a lesser degree, the Home Guard were used to help operate them. The 45th and 59th Royal Warwickshire Searchlight regiments and the Royal Artillery were also involved in protecting the city. Everyone worked together to search the skies above the city to spot enemy planes and ground them.

One particular incident happened in Earlswood in May 1941. One of the targets was the Austin factory at Longbridge. Enemy

*Cole Valley Road, Hall Green. 17 September 1940. This looks like a
normal street scene with people going about their daily business, until
you take a closer look at the bomb-damaged houses. Reproduced with
the permission of the Library of Birmingham.*

planes had been searching for the factory with no luck. One was
sighted just after midnight as it attempted to negotiate the barrage
balloons, and it was seen again somewhere around Acocks Green.
The Royal Observer Corps were on its tail, which alerted the local
searchlight unit, of which some fired upon the plane. The plane was
a German Heinkel and was allowed to carry on its path because
one of the guns on the ground malfunctioned.

The plane circled the area and was again fired upon but was
not brought down. Later, in the early hours, the plane returned.
Operating the guns was Lance Bombardier A.A. Hanson, who
had described the plane as being like a 'mosquito at a picnic'. The
plane was eventually hit. One crew survivor was taken to Solihull
Hospital and eventually ended up in Canada as a prisoner-of-war.

Such was the intensity and destruction of the Blitz in
Birmingham, it is beyond the scope of this book to detail every

single raid and the damage done. The first warning, however, came on 25 and 26 June 1940. The sirens were sounded and the people of Birmingham headed for the various shelters at 11.30pm. This, with huge relief, was a false alarm. It wasn't to be for real until 9 August 1940, when Erdington was bombed. Jimmy Fry was a young soldier on leave from the army, and he died in this raid, along with six civilians. It is thought that, as this area was residential, the enemy had mistaken it for one of the factories at Castle Bromwich, or Fort Dunlop. But for the people of Birmingham this was no consolation and proved to be a warning of worse to come.

They didn't have long to wait. On 13 and 14 August, the *Luftwaffe* hit their mark – Fort Dunlop and Castle Bromwich. At 11.30pm on 13 August 1940, the factory at Castle Bromwich was hit causing extensive damage. There were many people injured but few fatalities. It was too risky to continue any full-scale operations there, so manufacturing was moved to other airfields, including Cosford in Shropshire, temporarily. Although the Dunlop factory itself wasn't so badly damaged, some of the bombs landed in Sutton Park and Bromford, including the Rollaston Wire Company.

Another raid occurred on 15 August 1940, damaging parts of Yardley, Small Health and Acocks Green. The Singer factory was also damaged. This time, eleven people lost their lives, seven of whom were in a public shelter in Bordesley Green East. Over the next few nights the raids continued over the city, hitting the Castle Bromwich Aerodrome and Moss Gears Ltd, to name just two.

The Blitz was affecting how the local fire brigade operated, and their services were to become all the more important in dealing with the aftermath of the raids. Back in 1939, before the Blitz and the war took hold, Birmingham Fire Brigade released their annual report. They had been busy with in excess of 2,000 calls in the city, with a price of £175,000 (£10,805,495) estimated as property destroyed by fire. Of the 2,000-plus calls, seventy-two were deemed malicious, and there had been 649 calls for chimney fires.

They had even estimated how much time had been spent at calls – 1,280 hours, with almost 28 miles of hose utilised. The most serious fire at the time had been at the Birmingham Small Arms Company (BSA) works on 4 July at Armoury Road. There was also the Auxiliary Fire Service in the city that had attended 200 fires. Forty of the force were on active service. There would be

Interior of public air-raid shelter, Newton Row, Aston. 26 August 1940.
Shelters were not always the safest place to be. Reproduced with the
permission of the Library of Birmingham.

many more fires to come during the Birmingham Blitz, and the
fire service would be stretched to its limits.

Those risking their lives for the civil defence of the city were
admired and often thanked by way of church services and other
events. There was such a service held at the parish church with
the lord mayor and lady mayoress in attendance. It included a
parade, starting at the municipal car park, that wound its way
proudly through the city with the lord mayor taking the salute at
the Market Hall. The Rector of Birmingham, in his sermon, spoke
about the need for 'vigilance, patience, efficiency and discipline' in
the work those involved in civil defence did.

The ARP (air-raid precautions) wardens also took part in
many demonstrations and training throughout the war. One

Exterior of Bournville Lane Public Shelter. 14 January 1941. Reproduced with the permission of the Library of Birmingham.

such occasion saw 1,000 ARP wardens who were attached to the Birmingham 'E' Division East attend Warwick Cinema at Acocks Green to watch an instructional play called *The Raid*. It was set in a warden's post with sound effects of bombs and aeroplane engines. It was authentic with bricks and bits of wood raining down. The audience was instructed to see how the First Aiders went about attending to casualties, including men pretending to be trapped under fallen masonry. They were given a running commentary on how the injuries were assessed and the casualties treated.

There was also a little light-hearted article in the *Birmingham Mail*, Wednesday 10 January 1940, which told of potential unusual recruits to the ARP service. Entitled 'Nature's Air Raid Wardens', it told the lovely story of how, in the past, because pheasants fly off in response to both the sound of gunfire and thunder, they could

Rowlands Road, Yardley. 5 September 1940. Note the twisted Anderson shelter in the garden. Reproduced with the permission of the Library of Birmingham.

warn people of an approaching air-raid. This was first suggested by prominent zoologist W.B. Tegetmeier in 1881, who discovered the birds had a more acute sense of hearing when it came to such sounds. It was claimed that during the Great War, pheasants had saved people's lives in many towns in Great Britain and on one occasion alerted people in Wolverhampton to an approaching zeppelin. It was now being mooted whether to keep pheasants in public parks and gardens.

The police force was placed under pressure during the war, particularly with the Blitz, and many police officers were killed or injured in the course of their duties. One policeman, Constable B224 Harold Lewis, was killed when a bomb fell between

Bradford Street. 19 October 1940. Needles and pins manufacturers.
Reproduced with the permission of the Library of Birmingham.

Colmore Street and Bristol Passage in Bristol Street on Saturday 23 November 1940.

Another police officer, PC B247 Walter Hudson, who was a reserve constable at Bristol Street Station, was on duty that day when he heard a noise and came out to find Harold on the floor, his head bleeding with his helmet badly buckled still on his head. He was pronounced dead at 12.50am that day. Cause of death was found to be compound multiple fractures of his skull.

The Blitz had a devastating effect on the city and it would be decades before the bomb damage was cleared and rebuilding commenced. They are even discovering unexploded World War Two bombs in the city today. Recently, a 550lb bomb was uncovered in Aston by some unsuspecting workmen. The area had to be evacuated and so fragile and corroded was the bomb that it couldn't be moved and had to be disposed of, in situ, by way of a controlled explosion that could be heard and felt for miles around. Who knows how many more are just sitting there under the feet of the people just passing by? It's a legacy the people of Birmingham would rather not have had from Hitler.

ARP uniform buttons. Author's own.

CHAPTER SIX

Other Defences

From the beginning of the war, the government were concerned about Germany invading Britain, just as they were invading the rest of Europe. They needed a strategy and plan to prevent this from happening. One of the things they did to help counteract this was to form the Home Guard. These were primarily volunteers who would be trained up to defend Britain in the event of such an invasion.

Alongside the Home Guard, up and down the country, towns and cities were recruiting volunteers to help fulfil this vital role. In Birmingham, this consisted of the six sections of the city council's utilities departments with its primary aim of protecting those vital facilities. A Company was made up of employees from the council house offices themselves and B Company were gas employees, C Company water, D Company salvage, and E Company electricity. They had, at one point, a total of 1,210 men.

Alongside these men were volunteers from the city's other services, such as the transport works. From May 1940–July 1940 the 9th Birmingham Battalion (public utilities) local defence officers were in situ, which then became the 9th Birmingham Public Utilities Battalion Home Guard until October 1940. From then on, until December 1945, they were the 29th Warwickshire (Birmingham) Battalion Home Guard. Their commanding officer was Major T.B. Pritchett MC – the Lord Mayor of Birmingham – and then from 1940–1944 it was Lieutenant-Colonel E.V. Horton MC JP.

An announcement was made in May 1940 by Anthony Eden that they needed to form a Home Defence Volunteer group in Birmingham, and T.B. Pritchett asked for 'public spirited citizens' to take up the call. They needed to protect the city's infrastructure as much as possible. Other departments also made similar calls for volunteers from their own staff.

Anthony Eden, the 1st Earl of Avon, was in the British Conservative party and was initially Secretary of State for Dominion Affairs. Although he was held in high regard by the prime minister, Winston Churchill, he was not a member of the War Cabinet but did have special access to it so he could keep better communications between the cabinet and the dominions.

Prior to the war, Eden joined the Territorial Army with the rank of major, but when war was declared, instead of mobilising he returned to the government. When Churchill became prime minister in 1940, Eden was appointed Secretary of State for War, later returning to the Foreign Office as a member of the committee of the political warfare executive, leader of the House of Commons in 1942, and as prime minister from 1955–1957.

The war affected Eden both professionally and personally. Tragically Simon, his eldest son, who had served in the war as a navigator in the RAF, went missing in action in Burma in June 1945 and was declared dead. Then Eden's marriage ended.

Initially, the response to Eden's request in the city was good, which led to waiting lists and the production of more enrolment forms as they had run out. Many of the volunteers had some previous military experience, but some did not. It was a bit of a shambles to begin with. There was a lack of uniforms and basic equipment, so their initial training was done using whatever they could muster together as alternative weaponry for the first few weeks.

Then the city saw the identification of its most vulnerable points with guards organised to protect them in shifts. The guards' main duties were to prevent sabotage of the city's vulnerable points, guard the works and buildings identified as vulnerable, and prevent invasion from enemy forces. There were nineteen vulnerable points identified, snaking down from the Eden Valley in Wales all the way to Hams Hall in Warwickshire.

It had already been identified that due to the positioning of Birmingham geographically and the nature of its important war-work, it was the ideal target for enemy forces. If the Germans could bring Birmingham to its knees, they would be one step closer to winning the war. The valuable role of the defence forces of the

Home Guard should never be underestimated. Without their vigilance and challenging work, the outcome of the war could have been very different. Night after night they put their lives on the line to protect the infrastructure and the city's inhabitants. Their training was intense. Some of their NCOs gained qualifications in grenade instruction and were given permission to practice using live grenades. Other courses included signals, unarmed combat and intelligence security, anti-gas, and town fighting. At Frankley, in Bromsgrove, bordering the city, the water company had its own rifle range with the 39th Warwickshire Birmingham Battalion sharing another range at Mackadown Lane, Kitts Green, near where Ace Business Park stands today. They weren't the only company to have their own facilities. The Gas Committee had a private grenade range at Washwood Heath, approximately 2 miles north-east of the city centre, near Alum Rock.

When the proper weaponry did make an appearance, they used, amongst others, automatic and revolver pistols, Browning Automatic rifles and P14s, Lewis LMG and Browning MMG machine-guns with Northover projectors and grenades. The battalion even held a public demonstration of their capabilities in Adderley Park, which sits in the east of the city. In 1855, Charles Adderley MP gave the city 8 acres of land, which formed the park.

Things did not go to plan, however, with some of the grenades that had been fired at an ash heap becoming lost, requiring volunteers to go and retrieve them. The commanding officer arrived to supervise proceedings with his pocket full of half-crowns and beer in his car. It took four hours to find the grenades, after which the beer was drunk. The battalion also went to many of the city's parades and functions.

One of the platoons was attached to the regular army and went to Dover for training. The men in the platoon were taken from all companies and were commanded by Second-Lieutenant H.H. Williams of B Company, supervised by Major R.H. Rawll. They were attached to the 2/7th Battalion of the Royal Warwickshire Regiment, and their posting was seen as a real advantage when it came to training, which could only benefit the city. Their posting was also around the same time as the enemy launched their vicious and destructive V1 flying bombs, which certainly made life at Dover and in the Citadel where the platoon was based interesting.

A Company had Major L.M. Abbot in command and Captain F.F. Radford as second-in-command. The warrant officer at the time was Company Sergeant Major J.T. Cotton. They had 450 men enrol and were responsible for protecting the council house, the council house extension and the civic centre – the heart and lifeblood of Birmingham.

In order to fulfil their duties, they had to reduce the entrances into the buildings and cordon off various areas with fences to control who had access to the public areas. They also achieved this by introducing interview cards and special passes for members of the public who requested entry. There were armed guards at these entrances, with guards situated outside also undertaking patrols. Vigilance was key. The first guard postings here happened on 24 June 1940, and they had truncheons until other weapons became available.

From July 1940, they were taken into the 9th Birmingham (Public Utility) Battalion and formed the 29th Warwickshire (Birmingham) Battalion in October 1940. Interestingly, and somewhat surprisingly, they initially used some antique weapons from the city museum. These included elephant guns and Flint-locks, although using the Flint-locks were not without hazard, as they had the capacity to damage hands. The council house held civic dinners and ceremonies for some quite distinguished guests. They mounted guards of honour for such guests as King Haakon of Norway and General de Gaulle.

B Company was made up of five platoons, who had responsibility for protecting the gas works at Windsor Street, Nechells and Saltley, near the centre of Birmingham, wagon repair shops, Washwood Heath Gasholder Station and the Fittings Department in Lord Street. They were commanded by Major A. Bradbury, with Captain J. Bithell MM as second-in-command. But the company had a major problem. Making gas was time-consuming and had to occur round the clock, which presented them with problems of guarding and recruiting volunteers as the employees had to work shifts and there were always workers on site. They also had to make sure that the fire service was adequately maintained, although 700 men did volunteer.

Civitas sine aqua Civitas non est. A city can do without many things but without water it cannot survive. This was the motto of the water company that made up C Company. The company was headed by Major A.E. Fordham and Captain J.L. Tyler MM, and they covered the vulnerable points of Frankley Reservoir and Bartley Reservoir in the city itself, and the Elan Valley and Elan Aqueduct in Wales. When it is considered that the Elan Aqueduct is approximately 73.5 miles long, it can be appreciated that the manpower needed and the protection of this feature was not easy. By June 1940, 183 water company workers had enrolled with a total of 298 covering the other areas.

C Company had small arms training and were renowned for their musketry, having had the advantage of a rifle range at Frankley. They won all events in the musketry competition in 1944. There were many courses that members could undertake, but the most popular were Proficiency and Skills at Arms badges. In addition to these courses, they also attended two camps at Frankley in 1942, alongside a couple of camps at Whittington, between Lichfield and Tamworth in Staffordshire. They were keen to work together and every night they were on duty they liaised with military personnel, the barrage balloon operators, other Home Guard companies, the police, ARP and First Aiders, amongst others.

D Company was made up of volunteers from the salvage department. They had five platoons and, under the command of Major W. Teare and Captain Williams, were responsible for various works across the city, including Montague Street in Tyseley, Rotton Park Street in Lifford, and Brookvale Road. When they first formed, there were 301 men, of whom ninety-five eventually left to enrol in the armed forces. At stand-down, 153 remained.

Musketry and anti-sabotage were the focus of this company and they were so good at musketry that they won the Annual Battalion Inter-Platoon Shield two years running (1942 and 1943). They also held camps, the first being at Hagley in 1941 with others held at Whittington. Being a part of these companies was not without risk and, sadly, three men of D Company, died whilst fulfilling their duty. The death toll also included two other men, civilians George Vine and Arthur John Weeks.

One of their many escapades included a particularly fraught event resulting in bomb damage from a high explosive that detonated just 15 feet from the guard room. The guard commander, on inspecting the damage in the morning, was perplexed to see some bodies, as he had not been aware that anyone was there when the bomb fell and so had not sought to send in rescuers. It wasn't until the sergeant looked further into the matter that it was realised where the bodies had come from. There was a forensic laboratory next door.

E Company were made up of men from the Electricity Supply Department, with orders to protect Hams Hall Generating Station in Coleshill in Warwickshire, and Nechells Generating Station in Birmingham. These stations were particularly at risk from the attention of the *Luftwaffe*. It was deemed so important to protect these stations that the War Office requested the formation of an anti-aircraft battery (72nd Light Anti-Aircraft Battery), with 111 men, mainly ex-service. The company soon grew to 303, divided into five platoons, each with two sections. There was one platoon on duty each night. One section covered Hams Hall and the other Nechells. Every man on duty had to do two-hour patrols, frequently whilst under attack from the skies both by enemy planes and inclement weather. It was reported that E Company did more guard duty per man than any other company.

These were not the only companies to be doing their bit to protect the city. There were plenty of other work places and organisations that also formed part of this guard at various points across the city. One of these was the Dunlop Rubber Company Ltd, which, in preparation for the event that the enemy would take out the telephone and telegraph systems, started a pigeon post. Photographic films little bigger than a postage stamp had messages on them that were attached to the legs of the pigeons. It's incredible that 35,000 words could be contained on just twenty-five of these films, which were read back by being projected onto a screen. Some of the pigeons came from the king's loft at Sandringham.

Similarly, the Transport Company also helped to protect the city. Birmingham, even back in the war years, covered a large area and, in order for trade and the normal comings and goings of everyday city life to continue, not forgetting the need for military and Home Guard and other personnel to travel the city, it was imperative that the transport system remained intact and efficient where possible. This is where the Birmingham City Transport Company came into their own.

This 3,000–3,500-strong company (the 31/32 Warwickshire (Birmingham) Battalion) had the task of protecting the nineteen depots/vulnerable points. Each unit was given a P number for identification. Initial training was Squad Drill and Physical Training, as they had to wait, as many other companies did, for equipment to become available. Then came the building of the assault courses at Perry Barr Recreation Ground and the Transport Stadium. They also had small rifle ranges that were in the inspection pits of some depots, garages and some air-raid shelters.

At one point, because they were desperate for arms, weapons came in the form of P17 rifles, at a ratio of one rifle for every seventy-five men, which had been in storage since the Great War. They caused some problems for the men tasked with de-greasing them and getting them ready for use.

One important exercise for the battalion was held at Cannock Chase on 12 July 1942. This involved the 32nd Battalion resisting giving ground in an attack by the 31st Battalion, which was not easy given the unforgiving terrain of the environment. They had camps, most notably at Bewdley, around 20 miles from Birmingham, and competitions such as Open Range Firing, won by P.27 (Acocks Green) in 1942.

The Transport Company also had an excellent band, of which some members formed a military band for the battalions. They were even featured in a BBC broadcast at the time. Aside from the band, they were also keen to engage in and promote sports. They held athletics events at the Transport Stadium, swimming galas and football matches.

The company was also keen to give to charity and, from 1943, pledged that all donations would be given to the Royal Warwickshire Regiment Prisoner-of-War Fund. At a football match played at Villa Park between Aston Villa and Birmingham City, a collection raised £150 (£6,481). Altogether, the battalion raised just over £1,667 (£72,034) for the fund.

The battalion also had welfare funds for each unit, which was to be spent on comforts for its members in the armed forces and for some Home Guard equipment. Their HQ had a similar fund that was contributed to via holding boxing matches and dances, etc.

Some members of the battalion received medals and commendations at the end of the war due to their contribution to the war effort. Sergeant G.H. Rowe of Unit P.34 (Selly Oak) received the British Empire Medal and was Mentioned in Despatches. Good Conduct Certificates were awarded to, amongst many others, Company Quartermaster Sergeant F.T. Law P.29 Unit (Perry Barr), and Sergeant A. Richards P.28 Unit (Harborne).

The Home Guard also had its own warship. Birmingham is probably the furthest you can get from the coastline, so how did it end up with a ship, and where was it sailed? It was a small humble motor-launch that travelled the canal network at Ladywood (which is where Chamberlain Gardens and Edgbaston Reservoir are now), with a top speed of around 10 knots. The factory employees at Ladywood Home Guard unit bought it.

There were many more members of the Home Guard covering Birmingham and the surrounding area. In fact, 50,000 men volunteered in the various units and it was a monumental task to co-ordinate such a vast scheme, which Colonel Woods took on with great leadership and organisational skills. They all worked together and alongside other agencies to keep the infrastructure and inhabitants of Birmingham safe.

Civil defence was uppermost in the corporation's mind and was the duty of every citizen. It would only take some careless talk on street corners or a light left on in a window for the enemy to gain the upper hand. One way the defence of the city manifested itself was the distribution of Anderson Shelters to around 105,000 homes in the city.

But just because the shelters had been distributed didn't mean

Another Birmingham family who endured the bombings – Edna, June, Freddy and Ann Greaves with Howard Packwood. Notice they have implemented one of the strategies to try and lessen bomb damage by taping the windows. Courtesy of Jackie Sayle.

they were being correctly erected. It was advised that, in order for them to be splinter-proof and afford the best protection, they should be situated within 15 feet of a brick wall and, if there wasn't one, they should build an impacted earth mound at least 3 feet high. There should also be around 15 inches of impacted earth on top.

Another measure saw the transport system cease an hour earlier at 10.30pm and women began to be conductors on the city's trams and omnibuses, with increased fares and no cheap returns below 5d. Because Birmingham had such a good night life, patrons of the many theatres were reminded that the last public transport was about to depart by way of a curfew bell ringing in the theatres. Some shops were also forced to close earlier.

As there were many public air-raid shelters scattered throughout the city, they needed to find a way of allowing people to find their way to them in the dark during the blackout. The corporation began to look at ways the entrances to the shelters could be illuminated. At first, they used small globe-shaped lights, similar to those used in some shops at the time. But because they were so similar, it was feared this would cause confusion. So they experimented with an illuminated S-shaped box instead. People were expected, if they travelled to an unfamiliar district, to immediately locate their nearest public shelter, in case of emergency.

In the Tuesday 9 January 1940 issue of the *Birmingham Mail,* there were concerns about the financial burden that was to be borne by Birmingham Council. According to the finance committee, the cost of civil defence would be £1.8 million (£5,994,774,857) per year. In that year alone, the total cost for civil defence was estimated as £331,323 (£19,861,909), which they had calculated was equivalent to the average rate of 11d in the pound for each of the two years.

Alderman S.J. Grey, who was then the chairman of the finance committee for Birmingham City Council, said it was 'abnormal expenditure in abnormal conditions'.

The tasks and responsibilities of Birmingham City Council through the war years were immense. It was a large, industrial city, which was a target for the enemy and required a monumental effort to help secure it, as far as possible, against attack, and to help those who needed it when the Blitz came. The council made it clear that this was extra expenditure, above and beyond the finances needed for the everyday city services.

They had discussed the fact that there appeared to be no financial help from central government as far as air-raid damage went, but they were hopeful that the government would step up and agree that the whole country should be responsible for the costs incurred through rebuilding and repairing the city. Birmingham was, after all, an industrial powerhouse and, if Britain was to get back on its feet, the whole country would have to muck in and help.

The city had many visits from different dignitaries and officials throughout the war years. On one occasion it was the turn of John Anderson, the Minister of Home Security, who, staying as a guest at the Midland Hotel in the city, gave a speech on the issues he saw Birmingham having with its defence.

Anderson acknowledged that many factories in the city were in the business of producing munitions and other items for the war effort and that they were 'highly vulnerable' to attention from the *Luftwaffe*. But this wasn't the full extent of Birmingham's contribution. There were those trades and businesses that were trying to keep the home front going too, and those still engaged in the export side. John Anderson thought that those were equally important and could mean the difference between victory and defeat.

Anderson also spoke about the men who would be temporarily giving up their civilian life to enlist in the forces and recognised the strain this would put on those factories, trades and businesses who were expected to carry on with a significant part of its workforce away – except those businesses deemed of national importance and exempt from losing their workers. There was a balance to be struck, but he felt the city should be 'prepared for any frightfulness which our enemies may decide upon'.

His remit was that the city should pull together with greater co-operation between those in charge of business and industry and the local authority. When it came to volunteers, he was adamant that they should be compensated for any civil defence duties they did that meant they lost money from their ordinary employment.

Keen to see how the city was preparing itself Anderson, along with the Earl of Dudley, Alderman S.J. Grey, E.L. Payne and L.P. Lord, two directors of the Austin Motor Company, undertook an inspection of the new air-raid shelter at the Austin Motor works at Longbridge. At the time, this shelter was of a modern design and the only one of its kind. Carved into the side of a sandstone hill, it was designed to accommodate 10,000 to 11,000 employees. Compared to some shelters, it offered a little more comfort. It housed an air-conditioning plant, amplifiers that were connected to a control tower, and electric lights.

Following this ARP demonstration at the municipal car park, from which he was then shown the housing for those staff stationed at the depot. It was a full-on event. He saw ambulances, decontamination squads, stretcher-bearers, drivers and attendants, wardens, First Aid posts and the Auxiliary Fire Service. A big city needed major organisation.

In order to give Mr Anderson a realistic idea of how they operated, he was taken to the Old Flour Mill, Vincent Street, Ladywood. There, two live incendiary bombs were detonated to showcase the ARP's skills and how well trained the women volunteers were in coping with this kind of scenario.

Not only was the Austin Motor works' air-raid shelter unique, but Birmingham Civil Defence had another ace up its sleeve. The rescue party that had come to help were transported there in a specially constructed and adapted truck that had originated as a 35hp car. The vehicle could seat up to ten people and boasted all the essential equipment, including a telescopic ladder on the roof and a trailer.

With the Blitz came many fires in Birmingham, but bombs were not the only cause. One factory in Smethwick that was home to P. Fogwel Ltd, but owned by Smethwick Drop Forgings Ltd, who made chair frames, was destroyed before enemy planes got anywhere near. Just after midnight on the dreadful night, the fire brigade was called out but it was too late and after a five-hour battle to save the building, it collapsed. The flames were intense and the glow was visible from the city itself. There were fears that the stables next door that housed the horses from an undertakers would be harmed, but they were removed to safety. The fire brigade had a hard enough job as it was before the war started, and when the Blitz started their resolve, experience and skill would be put sorely to the test.

The defence of the city, its buildings, infrastructure, amenities, factories undertaking war-work and its inhabitants, took tremendous planning, organisation and execution, requiring many hours, finance and manpower. They operated under immense difficulty and danger, in hazardous circumstances, fully aware that what they were doing was as important as that of the armed forces and that by undertaking such work, which was, essentially, to help protect and preserve life, they were risking their own lives.

CHAPTER SEVEN

Life in War

Although many children were evacuated from Birmingham, some stayed behind with their families. Many people also lived and worked in the city and getting out to a place of safety wasn't really an option. Mothers were afraid to let their children go to strangers.

But what was life like for those who remained? With the daily threat of air-raids and the bombings that took place throughout the city, the pressure was immense. Every day and night, those who worked and volunteered for the defence of the city and to keep the city's wheels and businesses running placed themselves in extreme danger. While the rest of the city's population was getting down to work, taking part in the various local and national initiatives to help the war effort, such as cutting back on food and fuel consumption via rationing, growing their own vegetables and the war on waste, they were also at constant risk of the bombing raids that devastated the city.

One such family who had lived in Birmingham since the 1880s was the Wakelings, originally from Hockley. Part of this family was Mabel Owen, who originally ran the off-licence at 85 Hingestion Street at Brookfields, Birmingham, but had previously managed the Hope and Anchor pub at 79 Caroline Street, Hockley, with her then husband Alfred Owen. When he died, she couldn't carry on as manager so moved to the off-licence.

Unfortunately, tragedy was not far away. Alfred James Wakeling eventually took a tenancy at a local pub called the Vine Inn at 96 Carver Street, Hockley, with this, his second wife, Mabel. One night, 12 December 1940, sirens sounded and the city was pummelled by bombs. Alfred's brother owned a greengrocer's shop in Spring Hill and was told by a passer-by that the pub had been hit.

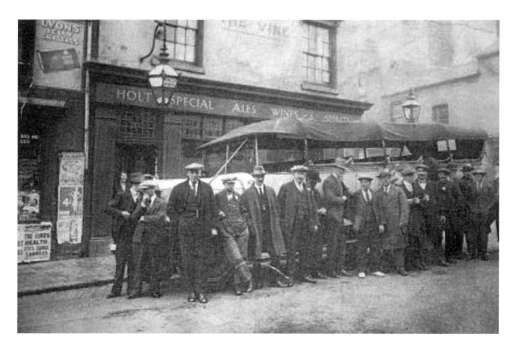

The Vine Inn, Carver Street, 1936, which was bombed in 1940. Courtesy of Jacqui Fielding.

Sadly, Alfred's body was found nearby with a woman presumed to be his wife, Mabel. In fact, the Birmingham Hospital Contributory Association Emergency Hospital Scheme, which kept records for relatives of fatal casualties, had a list (number 3) that was published at 9am on 13 December 1940, which stated that the bodies of Alfred (number 187) and Mabel (number 188) had indeed been recovered from the rubble of the inn.

The devastated family placed a death notice in the *Birmingham Evening Mail* on 16 December 1940, which read:

> *WAKELING – Alfred James, also Mabel (Late Mrs Owen) passed away (suddenly) in December. Will all Relatives communicate with F. Wakeling, Spring Hill, Birmingham.*

You will notice that the death notice doesn't mention that the couple were killed in an air-raid. This is because Birmingham was under a secret D notice that forbade anyone talking about the air-raids or revealing the level of destruction such raids had bestowed. This was an attempt to fool the German aggressors and not give away whether their bombing campaigns were successful or not. This applied particularly to the many factories and businesses involved in the war effort that were in the city.

One of the many slogans bandied about nationally was that walls have ears. Another was that loose talk could cost lives. The powers that be didn't want people's wagging tongues jeopardising the war effort. If the raids were reported in the newspapers, the location of such raids were kept deliberately vague and Birmingham was often referred to as a town in the Midlands.

Alfred and Mabel were buried together in grave number R-1260 at Key Hill Cemetery, previously known as the General Cemetery, in the Jewellery Quarter, in 1940.

Due to the number of casualties and fatalities, it was not always easy to identify them and mistakes were made. Descendants of the Wakelings discovered later, following the funeral and burials, that the woman Alfred had been buried with was not his wife Mabel. Her body was, in fact, found later, sitting in her chair with her knitting in her lap, in the rubble of the cellar of the inn. She had tried to free herself from the rubble, evident by the state of her nails and hands when she was found. She was, however, reunited with Alfred when she was buried in his grave, alongside the unknown woman, in 1941. Sadly, the family still do not know, seventy-six years later, who the other woman is.

An article that appeared in the *Birmingham Mail* in 2010 about the Blitz told the story of how a lady, Joan Randall (nee Lilley), contacted the family as she too had been in the city during the Blitz and wanted to attend the seventieth anniversary at the council house in Birmingham.

When the air-raids came, Joan's family had taken refuge in the catacombs of Warstone Lane Cemetery. Her sister wouldn't go there so instead walked to a relative's house. She had walked past the demolished pub and been frightened as she'd heard 'distressing sounds' coming from the rubble. She ran back to her family and they told the ARP officer, as they were concerned someone might have been trapped. But because the funerals had already taken place of Alfred and Mabel, it wasn't thought that anyone else was at the inn. The police were called, though, and this was when Mabel's body was discovered.

At the time of their deaths they had only been married for seven weeks. Theirs was a second marriage for both, which is why Mabel was still referred to by her previous name (Mrs Owen) in the death notice of the paper.

From the same family, Jean Booth, who was only a small child when war broke out, lived in Legge Street, Aston, with her father and mother Thomas and Nell Booth. When the air-raid sirens sounded, they would go to the Midlands County Dairy, which was situated almost opposite the fire station. Once, as they running to safety, Jean lost her shoe, but there was no time to go back and retrieve it.

Eventually Jean, her sister Doreen and their cousin Jean Rigby were evacuated with their

Alf, Doreen and Jean Booth. Courtesy of Jacqui Fielding.

school Bishop Ryders Primary School, Gem Street, Birmingham. The trio were sent to a farmhouse to live with two sisters who had also taken in two more evacuees. They were expected to work on the farm, including housework, before they went to the local school. Jean's job was to peel the potatoes. Unfortunately, one day the potato peeler went missing. It had been mistakenly thrown away with the potato peelings. The sisters blamed Jean and her punishment was to be locked away in bed all day without food or drink. Life was hard for a lot of evacuees and not all carers were as kind to their charges as their parents would have liked. Jean's sister and cousin, however, came to her rescue by throwing her cherries through the bedroom window.

The guilt of the punishment resting on the shoulders of the wrong child proved to be too much for the real culprit,

Nell Booth. Courtesy of Jacqui Fielding.

who confessed afterwards, and Jean was given a shilling by the farmhouse sisters. The evacuation process and being away from their parents affected some children for years after they returned home. Jean had nightmares of being lost and searching for her mother and sister. Many families such as the Booths lost all their family papers, photographs and heirlooms in the Blitz too, but this was a small price to pay when others who weren't so fortunate lost their lives.

Jean and Doreen had another sibling, a brother called Alfred, who stayed at home with their mother Nell. During one air-raid their house was hit, but all occupants escaped unscathed. It was always a risk remaining in the city, but some parents felt their children were too young to be sent away.

Just because there were air-raid shelters dotted throughout the city didn't mean that all its inhabitants made use of them. Nell's father Albert Bishop lived next door and often refused to accompany Nell and her son to the shelter. This proved to be a great stress for Nell, as she couldn't risk staying at home when she had her child to consider. One night, during an air-raid, when her father had stayed behind, the house was hit but her father was unhurt. They unfortunately lost everything else, clothes, furniture and house, so they went to the Delicia Cinema, Gosta Green, Aston. This is where Aston University now stands.

Communications at the time were sketchy and often unreliable, so when Thomas Booth returned from fighting in the war, he discovered that his family were no longer in Legge Street because the house didn't exist anymore. He found out they had moved to Herbert Road, Small Health, so he boarded a bus but got off the wrong end of this long road and had to walk, carrying his kit bag. There was no one in when he arrived and he was disappointed not to have received the hero's welcome that his friends demobbed before him had told him about. His family had no idea he was coming home.

During the war, more than any other time, family was uppermost in people's minds. Many men were away fighting and many others, including women, were involved in defending the city and making sure things ran as smoothly as possible. This must have been extremely difficult with the backdrop of the Blitz.

Another family, the Traceys, also had some interesting occurrences during the war. They lived in Teignmouth Road, Selly Park. There was Mr Tracey, Mrs Tracey and two sons, Bernard and

Bernard (older boy) and Peter (younger boy) Tracey. Courtesy of Fran Tracey.

Peter. One of the boys, Bernard, was born in 1931, his father having fought at the Somme in the First World War, but then worked on Route 36 (Cotteridge) as a tram driver. Bernard attended St Edwards RC School and Aston Commercial. Although life was simple, it was good, and they remember it being a quiet area with a big park to play in. It was a time when there were still horse-drawn milk floats and a blacksmith's. They lived in a three-bed terraced house with an outdoor loo near to the Ariel Motor Cycle Company factory and the Cadbury and Bournville factories, with various small businesses and trades in Selly Oak. Just before war started, the family moved nearby to a house with a shop, but the father started building a shelter before they left.

Because they owned a shop, when rationing came in they had to deal with the Ministry of Food on behalf of their customers and themselves. This was not something they were particularly happy with and they have had a healthy distrust and disregard for

Gordon F. Gilbert from Massachusetts, USA. He was a soldier the Tracey brothers befriended in Selly Park Recreation Ground during the war. Courtesy of Fran Tracey.

authority since that time. One benefit of having the shop was that the children enjoyed more sweets than those who did not have a shop. This was more than enough compensation in the eyes of the Tracey children.

Because of the threat of bombing, the family constructed an Anderson shelter at the bottom of their garden. The younger brother was a poor sleeper and had come downstairs one night with Bernard behind him. He would be half-asleep, but standing in the yard, waiting to go into the shelter. Often they would shelter under the stairs, the mother and two boys, as their father would be at work. Sometimes they were joined by an aunt and grandparents. His aunt was a fire warden on top of Grey's, a drapers/department store in the city centre. Once a bomb hit Selly Oak Park, very close to their row of houses, but they were all uninjured.

One evening the children were taken from the shelter to see the night sky aglow over Coventry when it had been hit by bombs. The children, following the bombing raids in the city of Birmingham, would go on the hunt for shrapnel and would be kept off school, which the authorities did not approve of.

Despite the dangers from the *Luftwaffe*, the Tracey children were not evacuated, although many of their friends were.

From the same family, Len Miele was born in 1934 and lived next door to Highgate Park in Balsall Heath. On the other side of the park was Rowton House, which was a working men's hostel, near Alcester Street. His father was Italian and worked putting down terrazzo, which is used for flooring, covering walls, etc. His dad had fought in the Great War but was too old to fight in the Second World War. Len attended St Anne's RC Infant School, which was next to the church he would eventually get married in.

At the time metal fabrication was a big industry in Birmingham, and because metal was needed to build aircraft, the railings outside his house and the whole row were taken and smelted down.

Because all aliens, those people from other countries who were not British, were monitored due to the risk it was felt they might pose to the war effort, some of them were interned. But the Miele family were not, although they knew of other families who had been.

The family remember the rationing and that there weren't many sweets around. As a substitute, they used to buy arrowroot from the local shop and chew that instead. They recall getting their rations of butter and bacon, but never complained. They also bought bones to stew and, because of their Italian heritage, they ate a lot of macaroni. To eke out their rations they kept chickens, which Len had to hold the wings of whilst his mother slit their throats. Once an incendiary bomb went off and set fire to the chicken coop, sending the birds into a frenzy. He remembered having roast chicken for a while after that.

The air-raid sirens wailed frequently and the family remember the factories over the road being ablaze. Len recalls being dragged, kicking and screaming, into the air-raid shelter. He recalled huge barrage balloons that were tethered to a truck in the park, but one became loose and the metal wire beneath it smashed the roofs of the nearby factory. He remembers walking up the steps of a shelter to go to the toilet, but a bomb hit the church over the road and he was blown back down the steps. The family were poor and Len remembers having a pair of boots given to him from Digbeth police station. They were known as Daily Mail boots.

His future wife May Hadley was born in 1936, but has a clear memory of a bomb going off one night that made the glass shatter in their dresser, which embedded itself in her sister's face. She also recalls a dead ARP man lying in the street outside. The things these children and many like them saw and the things they had to endure were terrible, and the images never left May.

Another local family had tough times. Aged 9 at the start of the war, Peter Webb, who lived in Sarehole Road, Hall Green, remembers that there had been warnings from Neville Chamberlain the year before that a war was coming. His father, Fred Webb, said that when Chamberlain made his famous speech about peace in our time, he could have sworn that Chamberlain leaned over to the journalists and said, 'I've got you twelve months.'

While life pretty much carried on as usual during this 'phoney war', the family had an Anderson shelter delivered. It was made of

Peter Webb in his plane with his mother knitting before the war. Courtesy of Lorna Webb.

an arch of corrugated steel. They had to dig a hole 6 feet by 6 feet and 2 feet deep. The shelter was then placed in situ, bolted together and covered with earth. His family slept in it at night before they were evacuated. His father made them a wooden frame with canvas stretched over it for a bed.

Peter recalls lying in that makeshift bed with his two sisters hearing the bombs exploding and the anti-aircraft guns and air-raid sirens going off, but he never felt scared. The only thing that did worry him at the time was the sound of his poor sister wetting the bed. He said he slept 'in the deep end!'

Eventually his father made two bunks for him and his wife at either side of the shelter. Peter said that when the bombs started to drop they would hold hands. It wasn't until years later that Peter realised how much danger they were all in. He knows now what a direct hit from a bomb would have meant for them all. They slept all night in the shelter, but some of his neighbours did not. Their attitude was that Hitler could do his worst.

Despite being a child at the time, he wasn't immune to the horrors that occurred all around him on a daily basis. He said that later his father-in-law would tell him about having to step over the dead bodies in the street and Peter recalls losing several school-friends to the bombs. Quite often when he arrived at school there would be children missing, which meant they had been injured or killed overnight. He remembers arriving at school one day to find the teacher's chair in splinters. A bit of masonry had fallen through the roof.

The school also had air-raid shelters built into the playground and the children would have drills to practise using them. They had gas-masks as well and during the drills a teacher would carry out a box of biscuits that the children were always hopeful would be opened. They never were as they were emergency rations. One amusing advantage to wearing gas-masks, Peter found, was that he and the other children could make rude noises through them.

The gas-masks still came in handy after the war to stop streaming eyes when peeling shallots.

He remembers that there wasn't much time for hobbies or interests and he recalls that his mother appeared to spend a lot of time queuing. If you saw a line you joined it as it often meant there was some food on offer at the end of it. If the butcher had some offal, this wasn't rationed, so they would often have stuffed sheep's heart or liver for tea.

Peter said there was a black market for food and some families did have cupboards full of illegal tins of fruit, etc, but not his family. It was felt that because the ships carrying the black market food had to be guarded by sailors and soldiers to allow them safe passage, many of them sank and if you dealt with black market food, you were also dealing with the deaths of those men.

He had a few close calls with bombs himself. One went off in the middle of Stratford Road, near to where he lived. The blast crater was so large that a Bailey bridge had to be erected so traffic and pedestrians could get past it. A Bailey bridge was a portable, truss bridge used a lot in the Second World War. It was made of wood and steel and came in light, easy-to-transport-and-assemble sections. The blast had also taken out the windows of some of the shops, but the shopkeepers just cleared the debris, brought their stock out onto the pavements and carried on trading.

Peter used to go up the Lickey Hills, near Birmingham, where you could get a good view of the vast expanse of the city. From there he could see the Austin Motors works brilliantly camouflaged to look like a row of houses. The company made armaments throughout the war. Another company, Peter remembers, is the BSA which, prior to the war, produced motorbikes. He recalls that Spitfires and other planes were produced at Castle Bromwich. Production was frenetic and Birmingham, already one of the leading strengths in industry across the whole country, was a huge workhorse powering the war effort.

Another large aspect of Birmingham was its theatres and cinemas, attracting big-name acts and actors. Peter's dad, Fred, worked in one such theatre at the beginning of the war before they were closed. When his father came back from the theatre late at night, his mum would run back into the house and bring out some food, often a bowl of stew, for him to eat in the air-raid shelter. One evening his father told him how he was cycling home from the theatre along Bradford Street when a bomb dropped not far from him and blasted him up the steep road.

He worked at the old Birmingham Repertory Theatre, Station Street, and was no stranger to mixing with some of the old greats of the period. One of his friends was Stewart Granger, who met

Fred Webb on stage. Courtesy of Lorna Webb.

his first wife at the theatre, and in order to avoid Granger's many adoring fans, they used to go down to the boiler room to eat their meals rather than the pub. The theatre moved to Broad Street in 1971, to the area now known as Centenary Square.

Peter's family lived through all the main air-raids on Birmingham, but it wasn't until eighteen months in that a bomb hit the water line, which meant there was no water in Birmingham. The water for Birmingham came from Wales to a reservoir called Frankley Beeches. Peter and one of his sisters were eventually evacuated to Loughborough in Leicestershire, around 40 miles from Birmingham.

One of his favourite pastimes during the war before he was evacuated and after his return on the way to school was to look for shrapnel in the streets. One of his friends found a melted wedge of metal with the end of an incendiary bomb still attached. The boy's father painted it with silver paint and they displayed it on their mantelpiece. Peter also had a good collection of shrapnel, but on

Horace Perks at Webley & Scott. Courtesy of Lorna Webb.

Horace Perks. Courtesy of Lorna Webb.

his way to school one day he was surprised to see the street full of feathers. Someone's mattress had been blown apart.

Peter's wife Audrey also remembered Birmingham in the war. She was one of triplets born to Horace and Ethel Perks and lived at Kingscliff Road, Small Heath. One of the triplets died. Stan, the other surviving triplet, and Audrey were 9 at the start of the war. In fact, the war started on their birthday. Audrey's mum would sit and cry as she polished the piano and the tear stains had to be polished over.

Her father was 38 at the outbreak of war and worked at the gun factory, Webley & Scott. The company, founded by William Davies, has been producing guns since 1834. When the Firearms Act came into force in the 1920s, sales dropped and they started to produce pneumatic guns too. Webley air rifles were used for training in the Second World War.

Both Horace and Ethel did valuable work during the war. Horace was an air-raid warden and Ethel worked as a nurse administrating First Aid in a factory in the day and tending to those injured in the Blitz at night. Because both parents were often out at night helping people. Stan and Audrey were left to their own devices and would sleep in an air-raid shelter under a tree in their garden. They had a close call when a bomber flying low opened fire, and they just made it to the shelter in time.

On another occasion, unbeknown to Audrey and Stan, an unexploded bomb lodged itself in the house next door. They had gone around the back to play in the garden and didn't realise that there was a bomb, with a policeman standing guard outside the front of the house. Suddenly there was a huge explosion with thousands of feathers floating around. Audrey wanted to stay and play but was dragged home by her uncle. She didn't realise until much later that the reason her uncle had been so adamant she should go home was the fact that the poor policeman had caught the full force of the blast and his head was in a tree with his helmet still on.

Terrible things like this happened all over Birmingham. The bombs were powerful and destructive and if a building scored a direct hit there was often very little to be done to save the occupants. Even the shelters, designed to protect people were often obliterated. Yet, even when faced with these despicable images and experiences, the people of Birmingham still carried resolutely and defiantly on.

Ethel Perks. Courtesy of Lorna Webb.

Horace Perk's drawing of a nut-cracker crushing a German bomb, which he drew during the war. Courtesy of Lorna Webb.

It wasn't just their mum and dad who volunteered to help in the war effort. When Stan was 12 he joined the boy scouts and was utilised as a runner between the mobile gunners, who were targeting the planes, delivering messages as to where to head for next. He found this scary in the blackouts, but realised he was doing important and worthwhile work. Both Audrey and Stan learned to knit so they could make comforts for the soldiers and sailors, although Stan refused to knit anything that wasn't khaki coloured or navy blue.

The family were also lucky enough to own an apple tree and the children would take an apple to school with them every day. The other children would wait for them to finish so they could eat the core – they were that desperate for fruit.

One day, already battered by the constant bombardment of bombs and the threat of death, the family were out on a walk and witnessed a German plane undertake a crash-landing in a nearby field. They rushed over to see if the pilot was injured. Audrey and Stan were given strict instructions to stay by the fence while Horace and Ethel ran over to the plane. The pilot had not survived and Ethel took the children home and contacted the authorities to give them the position of the plane whilst Horace stood guard.

Horace returned home with a parachute and a few tins of food from the plane. The food was eaten gratefully and the parachute was cut up in 1951 to make Audrey's wedding dress. Waste-not want-not was still in full swing then. Rationing and shortages didn't just end the minute the war was over. Although Audrey's wedding cake was three-tiered, only the top tier was real. The other two were iced cardboard.

At the end of the war the piano that had witnessed many tears was pushed out into the street and the celebrations began. Ethel was plied with drinks to keep playing. The glasses left rings on the top of the piano that Ethel was very proud of.

For many in Birmingham, life continued and people tried to make the best of a dire situation. Bread still had to be baked, the fields ploughed and the many trades and businesses in the city still needed to function, albeit, in many situations, in a new and fast-paced way.

The *Birmingham Mail* carried many adverts from such tradespeople and businesses requiring men and women to work with them. One such business, Chatwins Ltd of Tipton, stated that

Audrey in her wedding dress made from parachute silk. Courtesy of Lorna Webb.

they were doing work of national importance, casting grey irons, light or medium, and needed the labour.

The Austin Motor Company, at Longbridge, was also advertising for workers, wanting, for example, surface cutter grinders, gauge and tool inspectors, chassis erectors, fitters, welders, finishers, cabinet makers and sheet metal and iron workers. Because of the changing needs due to the war, many businesses across the city were forced to expand or diversify to meet the demands of industry and commerce.

Other businesses assured their patrons and potential customers that it was very much business as usual. England's had several branches in the city: 40–42 Corporation Street (ladies only); 30–32 Corporation Street (men's); and 66 New Street; including twenty others. They made a point of thanking their customers for giving them sixty-eight years of loyal support and said they were trying to 'play the game during these trying times'.

Even in the darkest of times people still needed entertainment, as did the troops abroad. In a piece published by the *Birmingham*

Mail in 1945, Captain Derek Salberg, who was one of the directors of the Alexandra Theatre in Birmingham, had been pleased to report back that many of those in the forces in Italy had access to the latest films that were also showing in the West End of London as well as being in advance of those shown in Birmingham. He stated that the troops tended to see at least two films a week.

Captain Salberg was home on leave, having been away for three years. He was happy with this but disappointed that many of the day's stars and entertainers hadn't been able to travel abroad to entertain the troops. On his travels, he had come across a lot of service men and left with the intimation that they were under the impression that the bigger names that did go out to entertain them often cut short their visits, claiming they had contracts to fulfil back home. The troops also had a contract to stay and fight for their country and were unable to get back home, often for months or years, never mind a couple of weeks.

On arriving back to the city, he was surprised by some of the many changes and restrictions that had been foisted upon them, either by the *Luftwaffe* or the government. One thing that irked him was the fact that soap was rationed, and also that it wasn't as easy to obtain hotel accommodation. One of the things he was hoping to do whilst back was extend the theatre, not realising the implications war had on the building trade in regard to a lack of manpower, resources and the need for strict monitoring and rules along with the now obligatory paperwork he would have to complete.

Although life was hard for many people, they still managed to live and carry on with their lives as best they could. The threat from Germany was constantly around them and they never knew if their loved ones away fighting would ever come back, or who they could really trust. Regulations and new orders were being brought in, seemingly on a daily basis, and it was all too easy to fall foul of the law. Yet despite these restrictions and dangers they took it all in their stride.

Programme of the Birmingham Theatre Royal, 1944. Author's own.

CHAPTER EIGHT

Keep Calm and Carry On!

No one knew how long the war was going to go on for or what the fighting taking place over the water would mean for those staying behind. When war initially broke out, on the surface there didn't seem to be much going on. The British government were concerned that the German forces were going to unleash hell from the skies. Their concerns were very real, leading to hospitals being re-organised and cleared ready to accept all the casualties they were expecting. This period of war was known as the Phoney War because, unlike at the start of the First World War, there was no fighting, initially, on the Western Front.

The people of Birmingham as, indeed, across the country, were given a false sense of security that maybe the war was over before it had started. But the government was keen to remind people that this was not the case by introducing the blackout and putting up posters that heralded the dangers that were present, even if the effects were not yet felt. It's no coincidence that after the blackout was introduced the number of road accidents and deaths increased as vehicles had their headlights covered with cardboard.

Although the people of Birmingham, at the start of the war, had not yet experienced bombing, their lives were affected in many ways, the most obvious being that some of their menfolk and workers had gone away to training camps and then were to be posted abroad to fight in the war. This meant, just as had happened in the Great War, that women were once more called upon to take on men's roles.

One of the biggest changes to life involved rationing. Because of the German blockades out at sea and with memories of food shortages from the Great War still fresh in people's minds, the government agency the Ministry of Food introduced the rationing of bacon and butter in January 1940. To obtain rationed food people were issued with ration books. These had detachable coupons inside that could be used in exchange for goods and food. Butter was rationed at 2oz butter per person per week. Other weekly rations per person included one fresh egg, 2oz tea and 8oz sugar. Each ration card had a serial number on it, with the owner's name and address. This took a lot of organisation and to help with this the Ministry of Food set up 1,300 regional food offices.

Rationing encouraged people to use food in ingenious ways. The war-cry of the housewife was 'waste-not want-not'. As war progressed and shortages really began to bite, they would use the ingredients they did have as a substitute for those they didn't.

It wasn't just foodstuffs that were in short supply. Petrol was eventually rationed for use in essential vehicles only. Clothing was also rationed, forcing flamboyant and fancy fashions to give way to plainer, more economical styles. There was even a shortage of tights for ladies who, unperturbed, used gravy browning to paint their legs, complete with a pencil line to give the illusion of a seam. Even furniture was not immune to rationing and it became practical rather than stylish.

The Ministry of Food were keen to show householders how they could economise and not waste food. They produced short films that were shown in the picture houses, demonstrating cooking and household tips to make rations go further. People were shown 'mock' recipes that imitated their family's favourite meals, including apricots being replaced with carrots in a tart and lentils and breadcrumbs to replace goose. Despite the rations, the population's health improved during the war years as they were eating far less processed foods and sugar, replacing them with wholesome vegetables.

The *Birmingham Mail* often carried recipes to help householders get the most out of their rations. One, concerning the rationing of butter, was an advert for Ryvita, which advised that instead of using butter, their product was just as delicious and wholesome with a scraping of marmalade, or with cheese that had been mashed with a fork and had mustard and milk added to it. They also suggested meat and fish pastes too.

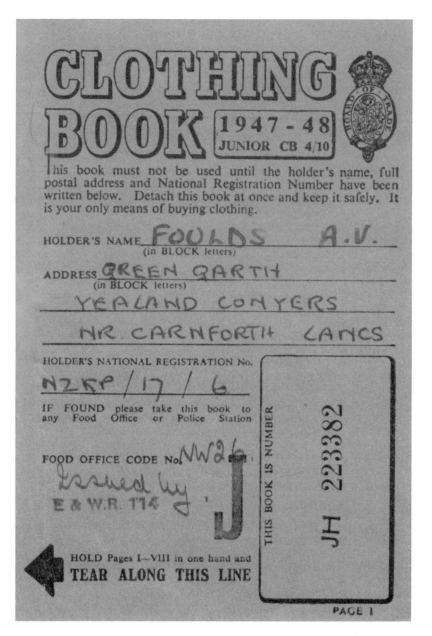

Example ration book from just after the war. Courtesy of Caroline Bagnall.

Rationing book, showing coupons inside, dating from just after the war.
Courtesy of Caroline Bagnall.

Poster showing how to reduce waste, from the Bournville Works
Magazine, *July 1940. Courtesy of Cadbury Archive, Mondelez*
International.

Another advert, this time for Ovaltine, claimed this drink to be 'The Best Answer to the Food Question', and made a point of stating that, just because there was a war on and food was being rationed, it didn't mean families had to do without a 'nourishing diet'.

There were also hints on how to get hens to lay more through the winter, mostly involving feeding them a wet and warm mash made of boiled-up household vegetable scraps and chicken feed mash.

The *Bournville Works Magazine* carried a section on helpful hints for its workers and housewives to implement in the home and garden. One article in the June 1940 issue had many suggestions on how to make money and resources in the home stretch further. There were ideas for substituting rationed goods, such as serving fried bread and grilled tomatoes with bacon to allow the amount of bacon to be reduced. Again, to reduce the amount of roast beef served at Sunday lunch, households were advised to add more Yorkshire puddings and stuffing.

They also had a dedicated Waste Prevention Committee, whose responsibility it was to see where waste could be avoided at the works and how they could use the waste that was unavoidable, rather than just disposing of it. Coffee grounds and old tins were put to good use, and the works' kitchen waste was fed to pigs. Even the waste raw materials used in the manufacturing of chocolate products, such as nut particles, were pressed so they gave nut oil that could be sold on to make soap and other products. Their waste reduction steps saw the amount of waste reduce from the pre-war amount of 28 tons to a more respectable 12 tons in July 1940.

The Ministry of Food were keen to inform readers of the *Birmingham Mail* just why rationing was important. The reasons given included: helps the war effort, ensures available supplies are equally shared, stops waste and helps in planning food resources and distribution. They likened the ration books to passports.

As with any new scheme, people had to get used to the new rationing system. It was made clear that householders should remember to take their ration cards with them when they went shopping as asking the shopkeeper to supply goods without presenting the cards was an offence.

It was reported in the *Birmingham Mail* that the first day of rationing had not been too traumatic and passed without too much trouble. But there were still people who had failed to register for meat and other rations who would find it difficult to obtain rations as the dates for registration passed. To make the idea of rationing more palatable, it was pointed out that not even the royal family were exempt and carried their own rationing cards.

Because so many people in the cities were made homeless due to the bombing, the Ministry of Food set up community kitchens known as British Restaurants that helped feed them cheaply. They were often to be found in church and school halls. The communities had no choice but to rally round and help each other because they never knew if they might need help in the future.

There were posters and leaflets and even broadcasts over the radio giving advice and tips on food, cooking and other household items. Rationing did not completely disappear until 1954. The war had had a huge negative effect on the country's economy, infrastructure and supplies, especially from abroad, and it took time to rebuild.

Across the country, various food-related companies and organisations were busy preparing for the war and making contingency plans on how they were going to continue feeding the

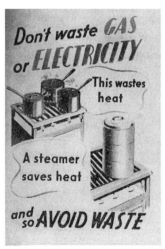

A poster from the pages of the Bournville Works Magazine, *November 1940. Courtesy of Cadbury Archive, Mondelez International.*

nation, given the potential shortfalls they might face. In January 1940, an advert appeared in the *Birmingham Mail* to let people know that the Ice Cream Association of Great Britain and Ireland (Inc.) was to meet on 9 January 1940 at 2.30pm at the Chamber of Commerce Building, situated in New Street, Birmingham. They were concerned with how the raw materials and finished products were to be transported during war-time and how they were going to source their ingredients.

When the rationing of sugar came into force, it was noted in the *Birmingham Mail* that nearly all its inhabitants had registered, but there was much haranguing of the 'laggards' who had failed to do so. Rationing didn't just affect householders. It applied to businesses like restaurants, cafés, coffee stalls and clubs too. Customers were entitled to 1/7oz sugar per meal and 1/6oz butter.

An advert in the *Birmingham Mail* for Cadbury's chocolates enticed customers to purchase their new 'Vogue' range of chocolates, which had flavours such as marzipan, tangerine, orange and caramel. Prices started at 3/- for a pound, 1/6 for ½lb, and 9d for ¼lb.

Meat was also rationed. Bacon and ham was restricted to 4oz if uncooked and 3½oz if cooked. There was due to be a new regulation enforced from 15 January 1940 regarding the control of livestock and meat. This was to come under the control of the Ministry of Food and there were to be collecting centres for livestock to go to. Prices would also be fixed. They ordered that from midnight 14 January there was to be no further slaughtering of livestock for food with the ministry taking this over.

The government were eager to ensure that people understood they should make changes to how they shopped and reduce the amount of waste they produced. Waste and overindulgence was very much frowned upon and seen as helping the enemy. In the *Birmingham Mail* in the 9 January issue, there was a piece stating that there were three ships. Ship one was loaded with necessaries and food, ship two had a cargo of munitions, and ship three was full of unnecessary products. People were advised to reduce their expenditure and consumption of the cargo in ship three to free up more space for more ammunition and essential goods. People would not only save money and help the war effort, but they could also plough more of that saved money into savings certificates.

Even the regional food officer Sir James Curtis made a request to housewives that they should do their shopping as early in the day and week as possible, to avoid busy times, and to remember their ration books.

Another war-time initiative was the introduction of identity cards. The National Registration Act came into force across Great Britain on 7 September 1939. It meant that everyone, including children, had to carry identity cards at all times. One purpose was to aid identification of bodies from the bombing raids. Everyone was assigned a special registration number that was on the card and included details such as name, date of birth, occupation and address. Each card was stamped and issued via the local registration office.

As war became imminent, the government arranged for the identity card system to be brought into action. As a matter of national security, they wanted to know who was living and working in Britain. There was great paranoia and worry about potential enemy spies and saboteurs who would put Great Britain in danger, thwarting their war efforts. The ID card was one way to help stop this. There was a National Registration Day on Friday 29 September 1939.

A lot of people across the country would soon find themselves moved out of the major cities and areas of industry, as with the evacuation to keep children safe. Women would be taking up a lot of war-work in the factories and many men would be enlisting to fight. There were also many foreign people living and working in the country that were now classed as aliens, and there were concerns that such people could potentially be a threat to national security. They wanted to keep tabs on everyone who could help the enemy win the war. With the prospect

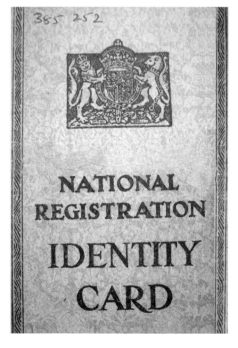

National Registration Identity Card. Courtesy of Mr Brightlee.

National Registration Identity Card. Courtesy of Mr Brightlee.

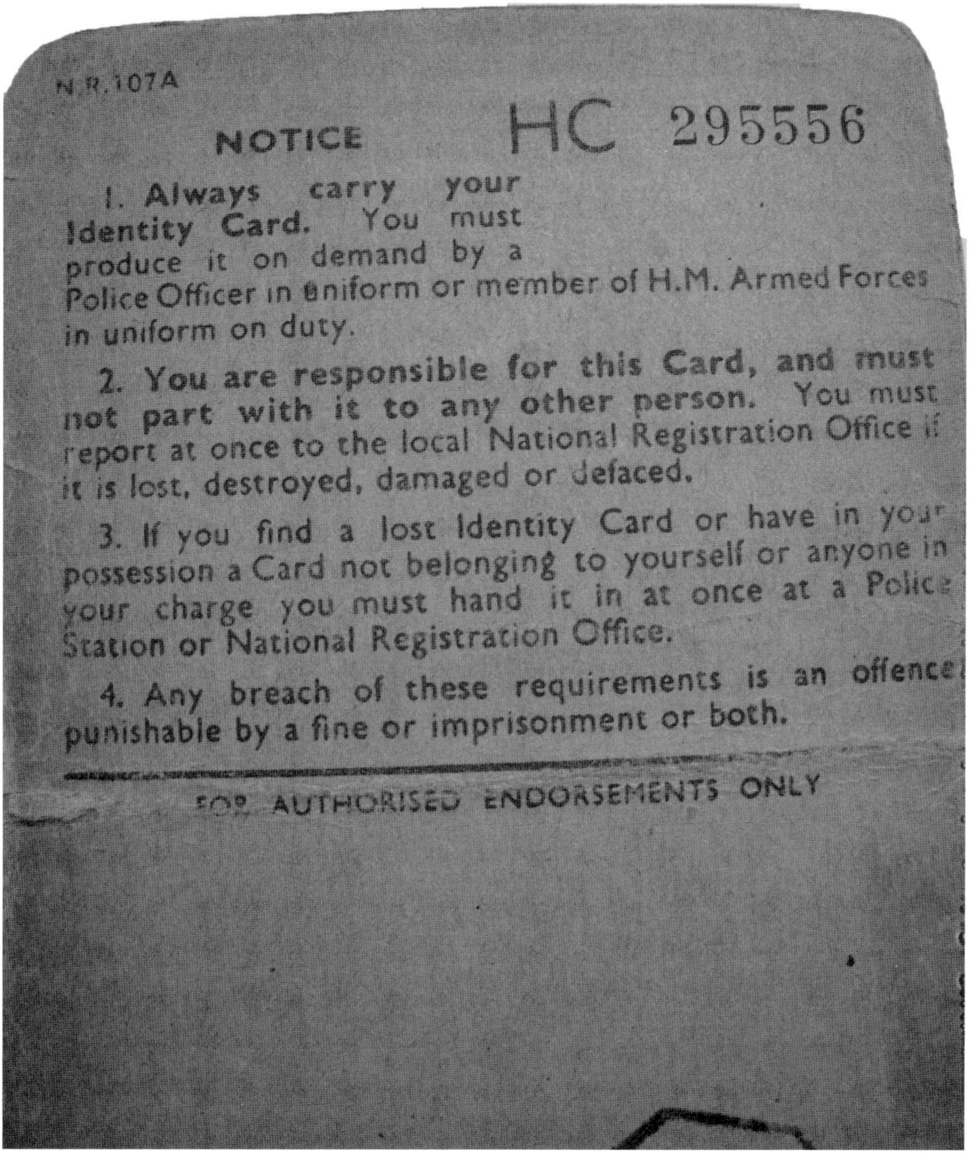

N.R. 107A

NOTICE   HC   295556

1. Always carry your Identity Card. You must produce it on demand by a Police Officer in uniform or member of H.M. Armed Forces in uniform on duty.

2. You are responsible for this Card, and must not part with it to any other person. You must report at once to the local National Registration Office if it is lost, destroyed, damaged or defaced.

3. If you find a lost Identity Card or have in your possession a Card not belonging to yourself or anyone in your charge you must hand it in at once at a Police Station or National Registration Office.

4. Any breach of these requirements is an offence punishable by a fine or imprisonment or both.

FOR AUTHORISED ENDORSEMENTS ONLY

Identity card, 1949. Courtesy of Michael Brightlee.

of rationing and the last census having been taken in 1931, they needed accurate numbers of the population so they could plan their war-time contingencies. If you didn't have an ID card, you couldn't get a ration book.

Early in the war the government also became concerned by people not of British nationality who lived and worked in the country. These people were deemed as possible threats to national security and it was felt they had the potential to be spies. The Board of Trade, therefore, made an order that stated that these people, including those firms and banks conducting their business in other countries, would be seen as the enemy. There were many people in Birmingham, as there are today, of many different nationalities and many were interned to protect Great Britain. It caused much inconvenience and upset, as these people had good friends and neighbours in the city who could not understand why they had to be taken away. It also created an atmosphere of suspicion and fear. People were reminded that careless talk cost lives and were encouraged to report any strangers or anyone of unknown origin to the authorities.

In all, around 46 million ID cards were issued. It was a massive but necessary undertaking and provided an interesting snapshot into the demographics and lives of the population from that time. It wasn't until 1952 that the cards ceased to be in operation.

With the growing pace of change, orders and restrictions, people felt the need to take refuge from the harsh realities of life. There may have been a war on but people still wanted to be entertained. As would be expected for a city, Birmingham was not lacking in venues for entertainment. Because it was a large city it could attract a few big-time names to its theatres. This was also true in the war years. People needed respite from the doom and gloom and deprivation of war.

In the 1 January 1940 issue of the *Birmingham Mail*, for instance, there were various adverts posted for pantomimes and plays, including *Babes in the Wood* at the Theatre Royal offering two showings a day at 2pm and 6.30pm. Over at the Prince of Wales Theatre you could watch Arthur Askey and Billy Bennett in the pantomime *Jack and Jill*, or if you preferred *Jack and the Beanstalk* you could head to the Alexandra Theatre. At the Hippodrome, there was the play *The Women* which, the promoters were keen to point out, had a forty-strong cast that were 'all women'. Prices here were 1/- to 6/-.

Other than the theatres there were also dance halls that the locals put to good use. At the West End Dance Hall, they were holding a Grand New Year's Ball at 3/6 per ticket. They also used entertainment to entice people in to help fund the war effort. Potential punters were promised 'fun and frolic for young and old' at the Lord Mayor's War Relief Fund Charity Dance to be held on 9 January 1940. There were to be two big bands, one of them Walley Dewar and his band with an 'all-star' cabaret. Tickets were 5/-.

There were also numerous picture houses like Lozells, which in 1940 was showing *Dramatic School* and Sydney Howard starring in *What a Man*. Situated at 54 Lozells Road, it opened in 1911 as the Aston Picture Palace but was demolished in 1922. It was then rebuilt only to be severely damaged during the bombing raids in 1941.

The people of Birmingham loved their dancing and so there were a string of dance schools scattered across the city. Frank Docker's School of Dancing at Queen's College Chambers in Paradise Street offered private lessons and friendly dances. Over at Acocks Green in the Public Hall were Bentley-Wall Dances accompanied by the Dixien Harmonica Band, with a special performance by Nina the Super Acrobatic Tap Dancer at a Grand New Year's Carnival, where those thinking of attending were enticed by 'novelties, competitions and surprises'.

If people were of a more athletic persuasion they could also go ice skating. The ice rink at Summer Hill Road offered three sessions daily, alongside exhibitions by Olive Robinson and Jimmie Thompson, who were billed as 'Britain's Wonder Skaters'. There was another rink at Sparkbrook called the Great Embassy Rink.

There may have been a war on but this did not stop Birmingham people from enjoying the many entertainments on offer. And if people didn't want to go out they could bring the entertainment into their homes. Scotchers Ltd, based in Corporation Street, were encouraging people to 'Let music lighten the blackout', by purchasing one of the array of pianos, radiograms and records they had in store.

The city also had a respected orchestra. They announced that from 21 January 1940, the City of Birmingham (Emergency) Orchestra was to begin their series of eight special concerts on Sunday afternoons, which would be held at the West End Cinema. This was to help 'provide relief from the tedium of Sundays in these war days'. Soloists in the first concert would be Moiseiwitsch and Arthur Catterall. Arthur hailed from Preston and was an established violinist and Moiseiwitsch was a Russian-born pianist.

Birmingham was also known for its art, but due to the war the city's art galleries had been closed. The Royal Birmingham Society of Artists were concerned that the city would lose out if the closures continued. As a solution, they organised a united artists exhibition to be held at the gallery in New Street. The exhibition would be opened by Professor Bodkin on 5 February 1940. Always concerned with charity, the society were going to donate 25 per cent of the exhibition's proceeds to the Artists' General Benevolent Institution that they felt would be adversely affected by the war with a greater pull on its resources.

Once the people of Birmingham had been provided with a little light relief from the war, it was time to get back down to the business of reducing waste and becoming more self-sufficient. Residents were encouraged to dig up their gardens and grow their own fruit and vegetables. Food waste was frowned upon and people were given tips on how to reduce it and cook using alternatives for ingredients. Powdered eggs became popular, as did using vegetables in cakes, for instance. Nationally, over the radio waves, the BBC gave advice on how to eat healthily with rationing with Dr Charles Hill. In Birmingham, the local newspapers gave advice with regular columns devoted to the topic.

Despite the efforts of the government to prevent it, hoarding and the black market soon took hold, leading to fines being issued. People had to queue for food. If you lived in the country you often fared better than those living in the towns and cities as there was more space to grow your own food and, if you could shoot rabbits and game and could fish, all of which were not rationed, you had a plentiful supply of food.

The Ministry for Agriculture were also busy making plans for how they were going to feed the nation. Many men who ordinarily would work the land had enlisted, so there was a shortfall of workforce, which the women, taking up the mantle, would go some way to filling. The ministry encouraged people to take the production of food quite literally into their own hands by digging up their gardens and planting their own vegetables and fruit. Local parks and open spaces were also dug up for the same purpose. Leaflets were produced showing people how to dig properly. There were demonstrations and leaflets on crop rotation and advice on which crops to plant when, and what was in season.

Due to the lack of supplies making it into the country, Britain became adept at making things out of almost next to nothing. The government encouraged people to patch up their clothing and household furnishings and other items rather than buy new. There were leaflets produced and demonstrations on how to eke out supplies. A good housewife was one who didn't grumble but used her initiative, and was resourceful not wasteful.

From the pages of the Bournville Works Magazine, *November 1940 – some land at Rowheath had been given over to grow savoy cabbages and broccoli for the works catering department. Courtesy of Cadbury Archives, Mondelez International.*

Not everyone entered into the spirit of rationing, however, and there was a well-known and popular black market going on in the background, where some people sold rationed goods. This was illegal, but people were permitted to swap items. Advertisements could be found in shop windows for items people had and what they wanted to swap them for. Bartering and negotiation were all part of the game.

At the time of the war, most women would have been no stranger to needle and thread and could make their own garments, just as their mothers and grandmothers had before them. But wartime saw them having to economise further and use their skills more than ever if they wanted themselves and their families to be adequately clothed. A lot of fabric was also needed for the armed forces for uniforms, so material became scarce. Adults' clothing was often cut down to children's sizes and people darned and patched their clothes.

Posters were produced urging housewives to 'go through your wardrobe' and instead of throwing old dresses out they could use their imagination and use the material for other things, or make them last another year. People also used things like wooden crates that the greengrocers had their fruit and vegetables delivered in as make-do-and-mend furniture. Metal saucepans were collected and melted down to help provide metal to turn into the wings of fighter planes. Nothing was wasted and to be thrifty and ingenious was seen as a great asset to the war effort, thwarting the enemy's plans.

Housewives were advised to keep the stockpot running and that most food waste including bacon rinds, bones, gravy, giblets and vegetables could be added.

They were also given hints on how to unravel wool clothing to be rewound and knitted into squares for blankets for the armed forces. It was to be unpicked, the wool was to be wound around the back of a chair and tied together with different coloured wool to be washed in warm soapy water, after which it should be hung up to dry and then rewound into balls ready for knitting.

There were lots of ways that the people of Birmingham were encouraged to help the City Corporation during the war. One such way came in a plea featured in the 1 January 1940 issue of the *Birmingham Mail*. The corporation wanted people to help paint the kerbs outside of their homes white to enable pedestrians and road users to see better at blackout time. Having already painted approximately 350 miles of kerb, the corporation was keen to point out that it would be too costly and time-consuming a job for them to do every kerb in the city.

On conferring, the chief constable of Birmingham and the city's engineer devised a plan where people would be asked to paint both the vertical and horizontal faces of the kerbs for a distance of 1 foot, with a foot's break between each section. It would be costly because they couldn't use ordinary whitewash, only the best enamel paint, to give durability, would do. It was also proposed to paint white bands around trees, lampposts and any other object that could be considered dangerous if it could not be seen in the dark. Citizens were encouraged to ensure that their hedges that bordered footpaths were kept trimmed to prevent injury to pedestrians, who may inadvertently wander into them in the dark.

Despite the war, life had to carry on as far as was possible and sport was no exception. Sport in Birmingham was big business. They had their football – Aston Villa and Birmingham City, alongside many other local clubs. There was tennis, cricket and rugby seeing many regular fixtures and games played across the city.

In war-time, sport continued but, as one commentator observed and wrote in the *Birmingham Mail*, it was inevitable that with many men away fighting or taking on APR duties and suchlike, spectator numbers dwindled. Association Football was affected by the war. The commentator claimed that in a good season they would see almost 1 million people either watching or playing football, but since the war started the pitches and stalls were all but empty. He didn't blame the people of Birmingham because, he quite rightly pointed out, they were busy with war-work and couldn't be concerned with sport until they'd finished their jobs.

There were also quite a few national sports fixtures held in the city throughout the war years. One was the National Skating Association of Great Britain, which had organised for three of its competitions to be held at the Embassy Rink, Walford Road, Sparkbrook, on 4 February, 2 March and 16 March 1940; pair competition, Lancaster Cup for Figure and Free Skating, and the Devonshire Park Bowl. Another skating rink, Summer Hill Road, had the right idea. They billed themselves as the 'brightest spot in the blackout', but reminded potential patrons to bring their gas-masks.

Sports fixture at Bournville. 1940s. The first lap in the mile. Courtesy of Cadbury Archives, Mondelez International.

There was an announcement in the *Birmingham Mail* in January 1940 that if Birchfield Harriers were agreeable, Birmingham City Football Club would be playing their first matches in the Midland Regional Competition at the Alexander sports ground in Perry Barr.

At the time, when it came to holding large sporting events such as this, permission had to be sought from the chief constable. He had allowed ICI Metals and an Aston Villa team to play there the previous week, with a crowd of around 4,000. Birmingham City, whose ground at St Andrews had been off limits since the start of the war, were seeking permission to play there again. The chief constable refused as he felt the ground was at too great a risk of attack from the air. As a consequence, Birmingham City had to play all of their home games on opponents' pitches until at least 30 December 1940.

Boxing, ever a popular sport in Birmingham, also continued in war-time. In February 1940, boxers Alfred Harper of Aston ABC and Cyril Gallie of Cardiff Gas ABC, who was the feather-weight boxing champion, were due to take part in a return match for charity at the Midland v Wales tournament at the Tower Ballroom, Edgbaston.

One match between A Quinney, Wolseley feather-weight, and H. Lee of Aston saw the former beat the latter on points following a six-round contest, which was held at the Holte Hotel in Aston in January 1940. In the same competition, Aston boxer G. Hartley also won his welter-weight bout against fellow Aston club mate B. Brown, with another feather-weight contest won by another Aston boxer, J. Measley, against D. Drake from Imperial.

The local factories also got involved, with a boxing tournament hosted at the Longbridge Works by the Austin Amateur Boxing Club with Coventry (standard) Club. For this contest, there was

Cycling race, Bournville, 1940s. Courtesy of Cadbury Archives, Mondelez International.

excitement as A. Harrison and Midlands champion (1936–1939) and British Championships finalist in 1937 Joe Froggatt were due to compete here.

Swimming was also important, but the various swimming clubs across the city were worried about how they could continue in wartime. So high was the concern, that the Birmingham Association of Swimming were to hold a meeting for all its members at the Grove Lane Baths, Handsworth.

Even in light of all the horrors going on around them, Brummies retained their infamous sense of humour. The *Birmingham Mail* carried items, often light-hearted, poking fun at the enemy. In one such item they suggested a new definition of a dictator country, saying it was a country 'where everything that is not forbidden is compulsory'.

They also stated that Franco had received a new car that had the capacity to tackle a 1-in-2 gradient hill – suggesting he was going to have an uphill struggle.

People also needed a little light relief from rationing and all the new rules and regulations imposed upon them. Again, the *Birmingham Mail* didn't disappoint. They carried a cartoon depicting a man and wife sitting at the breakfast table, with the husband staring at a pathetic slice of toast, asking which side his wife had buttered it, as a jibe against butter rationing.

Another cartoon showed a husband and wife walking past a shop in the city with the wife eying up the luxury goods on sale. The husband shouts 'eyes right'. It was making fun of the recent prime minister's speech about people having to go without certain things that they will miss. Presumably, the husband in the cartoon wasn't going to miss the amount of money his wife usually spent.

Another quip was making fun of Field Marshal Goering. He was a German politician, military leader and a key member of the Nazi Party. Apparently, he had been bitten by a dog and it was claimed that this dog now gave the Nazi salute in his 'delirium'.

Propaganda also was at play with rationing and how it was portrayed. One advert for Meadow and Pearkes butchers compared German rations to our own, implying that the people of Birmingham were lucky to be getting much more than their counterparts in Germany. For instance, they claimed at the time meat and sausages in Britain were unrationed, but in Germany it was at 17½oz.

To keep Birmingham moving, education may have been disrupted but it certainly wasn't forgotten. Many schools, particularly those in evacuated areas, were closed for varying periods from July 1939. In January 1940, fifty-eight elementary schools had re-opened. Usually, in the neutral zones or those areas that couldn't be evacuated, the attendance at schools was 15,000. The city, at the time, had 132,000 pupils on its rolls, of which 70,000 lived in the city's neutral zones.

There was also talk of improving young and adult education across the city. It had been realised that many young men going off to war would not have had the opportunity to learn a trade or business before they went, which posed the question of what would happen to them when they returned and were demobilised.

The authorities in Birmingham were impressed with a plan Lord Derby had concocted to give courses in commerce to those young men who had left school but were not yet of military age. Dunlop Rubber Company offered scholarships to such men with a grant of £52 (£3,117) per year. The only stipulations related to age and current educational status. They had to be aged between 17½ and 19 by the start of the course, be in good health and of British nationality, but educated to matriculation standard or similar. This level of education meant they were eligible to attend university.

It was expected that most of the training would take place at Fort Dunlop and at the nearest depot to the students' homes, or at the various other service depots across Birmingham, Manchester, Leeds and London. There were also assurances that those men on the scheme would be released to fulfil their military duty when the time came.

The company knew that after the war a lot of men who returned would not be able to work in the industry and businesses in the city because they had no experience of it, and this was their way of ensuring as many men as possible had the opportunity to take up such training.

Birmingham played a huge part in the war effort, both abroad and at home. But it wasn't just the ordinary housewife and families that had to bear the brunt of war. Local firms and companies also felt the pinch.

PHONE:- BROADWELL 1355 (3 LINES)   TELEGRAMS:- "DRESSINGS, OLDBURY"

CONTRACTORS TO H. M. GOVERNMENT

CUXSON, GERRARD & CO. LTD.,

MANUFACTURING CHEMISTS,

V/L

SOLD TO   OLDBURY,   BIRMINGHAM.

Mr J Douthwaite
        Chemist
                Prudhoe On Tyne.

TERMS:
3¼% if paid by
2½%
(EXCEPT ITEMS MARKED NET)
AFTERWARDS STRICTLY NET.

NOT RESPONSIBLE FOR BREAKAGES.   ANY ERRORS IN GOODS OR INVOICE MUST BE NOTIFIED WITHIN THREE DAYS.
NO RECEIPT IS VALID UNLESS ON SPECIALLY PRINTED FORM.

WARRANTY for DRESSINGS

All Dressings ordered and invoiced as
B.P.C. are guaranteed by us to be of
that quality.
    Cuxson, Gerrard & Co. Ltd.

DATE 19th. Oct   19 42
FORWARDED PER
CARRIAGE   Post   OUR ORDER NO   F 9836
YOUR ORDER NO

Quantity	Description	Stock No.	Rate	Per	Purchase Tax		£	s	d
X 2 Dozen	Belladonna Plasters	M 71/6	5/6	doz		1	10	11	0
X 3 Dozen	½" x 3½yds Z.O. Plaster	Temporarily out of stock							
X 4 Dozen	1" x 1yd " "	M 14/F	2/-	doz				8	0
X 3 Dozen	1" x 3½yds " "	M 60/F	8/0	doz		1		4	0
1 Dozen	Thermoid Plasters	M 85/6	8/6	doz	1	5		8	6
					3	3	2	11	6
	X Less 2½% Quantity Disc. off £2/3/0							1	1
							2	10	5
	Add Total Tax							3	3
							2	13	8

NET

NOTE:- CARNATION CORN CAPS AND ALL
PLASTERS, STRICTLY NET INVOICE.

CONTAINERS CHARGED MUST BE PAID FOR - CREDITED IN FULL WHEN RETURNED.

*It was still business as usual. Invoice from Cuxson, Gerrard & Co Ltd,
manufacturing chemist of Oldbury, Birmingham, to J. Douthwait, chemist,
of Prudhoe on Tyne, 1945. Author's own.*

CHAPTER NINE

Bournville and Cadbury

If you ever have occasion to walk through Bournville where the Cadbury and Bournville factories are still operational today, you will not be able to escape the unmistakable aroma of cocoa and chocolate. The company has been producing chocolate products for almost 200 years and certainly had its problems and part to play in the war effort.

It was Quaker John Cadbury in 1824 who opened a grocer's shop in Bull Street where he sold his home-made cocoa and drinking chocolate, which he would make using a pestle and mortar. He was keen to provide his customers with an alternative to alcohol, which was frowned upon by Quakers, and the thinking of the time was that tea, coffee and drinking chocolate were far better for you.

Then, in 1831, he expanded the business by opening a four-storey factory in Crooked Lane. Their products proved to be so popular that they were producing sixteen varieties of drinking chocolate along with eleven different cocoas, including varieties such as Spanish, Fine Crown and Grenada. Their products could be bought as powder or a solid cake. The names of some of the varieties were intriguing, such as Iceland Moss and Homeopathic.

It wasn't until 1847 that the business relocated to Bridge Street. There were sound business reasons why this made sense. They were moving towards the centre of the city and they had access to their own canal that fed into the Birmingham Navigational Canal, which meant they could then access major ports.

When John retired, the business was given over to his two sons Richard and George in 1861. They were no strangers to the factory and process, having worked within the company for a few years, although at age 21 and 25 they were still young for all that responsibility of nurturing and growing a popular brand to be resting on their shoulders. This was at a time when other cocoa manufacturers were facing difficulties, with some going out of business. But the Cadbury family had been canny and saved some money from inheritance. But although it helped them, the business still went through a rough patch. With Richard taking charge of sales marketing and George looking after the production and buying side of things, their early days were far from easy.

In 1866, the company turned a corner when they adopted a new way of processing cocoa resulting in Cadbury Cocoa Essence, similar to how the Dutch were doing it at the time. It pressed out lots of the cocoa butter that, prior to using this technique, had to be left in and masked with additives such as starch. They were the first in Great Britain to use this process and their gamble paid off with sales increasing. Many children and adults enjoy Cadbury Easter eggs and the first of these was manufactured in 1875, including the Plush egg and the Satin egg, which were made of dark chocolate.

It's worth remembering here that Birmingham, especially within its industrial areas, was poor and little more than a series of slums. The Cadbury family, as Quakers as well as manufacturers, were keen to help improve not only the working lives but also the home lives of their workers too. When they had to find bigger premises again, this was high up on their agenda. They came across a place nestled between the villages of Selly Oak, Stirchley and Kings Norton. It was 14½ acres in size and perfect for their requirements. It had a meadow and a stream called the Bourn. Originally a small cottage was there and the site was going to be called Bournbrook after a hall nearby and the cottage. Eventually they settled on the name Bournville, and the workers found themselves better off away from the slums of Birmingham.

But George didn't want to stop there. He had a vision of the future for not only the factory but the living areas of his workers. 'No man ought to be condemned to live in a place where a rose cannot grow,' he said, and in 1879 his wishes began to take shape with the start of the building of the new factory, designed by George H. Gadd. They also built houses for senior staff and the foremen.

This was soon expanded providing, amongst other facilities, a field where workers could play sport, gardens, a playground, swimming pools, dressing rooms and kitchens. It was like nothing anywhere else in the area. Not only did the workers live in improved circumstances, they were also treated to works' outings in the country and reduced train fares for those workers who commuted from Birmingham, 4½ miles away.

In 1893, the facilities expanded into a further 120 acres of nearby land, where more workers' houses were constructed. In 1895, he built a further 143 houses. George's vision had been to not build the common tunnel-back houses that reduced light, so the new houses were built to a rectangular design with big gardens. His new village won him much admiration, especially from the Garden City Movement. Not only were the Cadbury family entrepreneurial, they were philanthropists too.

The Cadbury's chocolate bar we know and love today was first developed in 1897 and was made from the discarded cocoa butter, but we wouldn't recognise it now as the early bars were unrefined and coarse.

In 1906, Bournville cocoa appeared, followed by the appearance of Bournville chocolate bars in 1908. They launched Milk Tray selection boxes in 1915, during the Great War, with Fry's, another confectioner, being taken over by Cadbury in 1919.

Having been through the First World War and survived, in the early days of the Second World War the company were celebrating the 100th anniversary of George Cadbury's birth (1839–1922). At the annual meeting of the Men's Shop Committee, 1940, as documented in the *Bournville Works Magazine*, in a statement made by Mr Lawrence, there was talk about how as early as 1937 they had been making plans should war break out. They were concerned about Hitler's 'aggressive attitude' and his association with Mussolini.

They decided to draw on the experience of those workers who had seen the company through the Great War, taking on board the kinds of restrictions and substitutes for their raw ingredients that the company used. This information they took to the Board of Trade in an attempt to pre-empt problems that the war would bring for the industry. The headquarters of the industry for the war was the office of the Manufacturing Confectioners' Alliance based in London, and the plan very much looked at issues that could affect transport and supplies in war-time, these being primarily the shortage of petrol and the commandeering of transport vehicles for the armed forces and war-work.

They decided that something had to be done to prevent such problems as far as possible. This involved working together and the pooling of resources of similar companies. Between them, Cadbury, Rowntree and Fry's had around thirty depots, and these were to form the basis of the new system to make savings on transport. This would partially solve potential transport difficulties, but what about raw material shortages? They planned to make sure that in such an event the materials, such as cocoa, that were available would be equally distributed.

But it wasn't just cocoa that could be affected. There was also cocoa butter, sugar, glucose butter, oils and fats, which as we know were rationed during the war. Milk would also be an issue for the companies, and this was further compounded by the number of government agencies and ministries that sprang up in the war that the companies had to deal with. There was no one-stop for everything. This was a cause of much frustration, well-illustrated by Mr Lawrence's comment:

> *Some of us in recent months have spent a lot of time not only in London but in going to and from London at a time when the train service is restricted! It is one of the ironies of war which help keep us cheerful – just when we have to travel twice as much as usual we are only able to do so at half speed.*

As the war progressed the industry did indeed see most of their lines restricted and being rationed. Another issue was the problems they had complying with the blackout. There were difficulties disguising the factory to ward-off bombing raids whilst keeping the factory well-ventilated. The company had also been building and had quite a programme that had to be halted during the duration of the war. One thing they were sure of, though, was that they were determined to stick to their principles of value for money, good quality and fair dealing This was not made easy because of

Anti-waste poster displayed outside one of the works' entrances. Courtesy of Cadbury Archives, Mondelez International.

the war with their customers, wholesalers and retailers expecting different things.

Although the company were surviving, just, they were living a hand-to-mouth existence. They were keen not to be seen profiteering from the war and were concerned about the kind of country England would be when the war was over and their place, as a company, within it. Their vision was clear:

We want to see Bournville still maintaining its lead position in our own industry, and, indeed, in the industry of the country.

When the Great War ended, the company received over 2,000 of those men who had survived the war in employment. Their message was clear to men fighting abroad in the new war:

We must be ready to welcome back those who have left us and who are destined to leave us, we hope, only 'for the duration'.

So great was the contribution of Cadbury to the war effort in Birmingham that it is beyond the capacity of this book to examine every detail. One thing of note was that of their contribution to the Friends Ambulance Unit. This unit has its origins in the Great War and was formed as the Quakers' response to the conflict. They felt the current ambulance services would not be able to cope with the scale of the casualties from the conflict and saw the unit as a way for conscientious objectors to help in non-combatant roles.

The unit was reformed in the early weeks of the Second World War. They provided vital support during the Blitz, both on the ground and in hospitals, as well as working out in the field supporting at battlegrounds abroad, helping non-military personnel in special clinics based overseas, and helping refugees and those affected by the war.

Because the family were Quakers, the factory was very much involved in the unit with several of their workers engaging in this kind of war-work. They followed in the footsteps of workers who had also been in the unit for the Great War, several of whom were now on the Bournville committee, including the chairman Paul Cadbury, who was with the unit from 1915–1919, and M. Tatham, who was commandant of the unit from 1918–1919.

In the *Bournville Works Magazine* of January 1942, a report highlights the experiences of the unit in Finland and Norway, 1940–1941. The report did state that most of the work was being undertaken in this country, with nursing and portering duties, also in rest centres, public bomb shelters and emergency canteens. They emphasised the fact that just because the unit was not engaged in combat their jobs

Members of the Friends Ambulance Unit leaving London, 1942. Many of Bournville's workers were in this unit. Courtesy of Cadbury Archive, Mondelez International.

and training were not easy. The training for both men and women in the unit was rigorous, with the women being trained at a camp in Yorkshire and the men training in Northfield in Birmingham.

Basic training took many forms, including route marches, drills, firefighting and medical lectures. They were taught all aspects of relief and nursing work, field ambulance procedures and anti-gas protocols. Once their basic training had been completed, they moved onto more specialised training, depending upon which of the three main arms of the unit they were destined to end up in: hospitals, relief or foreign service. This could involve learning another language, social welfare or mechanics.

Once trained some of the unit went to places in Great Britain that had been bombed, such as Dover, helping casualties, rescue work and evacuating hospitals. Others went abroad to places such as Greece, Turkey and Syria, and faced bombing raids as well as being at risk of capture by enemy forces. Paul Cadbury's son Edward was in the unit in China.

The company had a War Victims' Relief Committee, which aimed to organise the financial needs of the ambulance unit. They took into account the food, clothing and equipment required, health care and education. They were pleased to report that the unit had progressed 'from the crudest form of emergency service into a well-based service capable of standing the strain of both the "Blitz" and boredom in a long war'. They were proud that the unit had strengthened the community spirit of those neighbourhoods it engaged with, which could only be a bonus for the war effort.

The aim of the unit was to '… serve wherever service is most needed, and help to relieve some portion of the vast world-wide agony of war, in a spirit of reconciliation and faith in the essential brotherhood of man'.

The company also tried to do what they could for war relief. One of their endeavours, ordered by the royal princesses, was to gift chocolate to French children. Two hundred boxes of assorted chocolates were sent from Cadbury's and Somerdale. They replaced the traditional decorative red ribbon around the boxes with a red, white and blue ribbon and a picture of the donors slipped inside.

They were also a depot for National Service Christmas Parcels. There was a team of ten women and eighty men who undertook the parcelling after 7pm, after the hospital supplies work had ceased. The parcels were sent to every employee who was serving. Different departments within the company also added extra treats for their members in service. For instance, Bournville Athletic Club and the Bournville Dramatic Society sent a tin of cigarettes for each of their members, and there were Penguin books too.

Several employees in receipt of these parcels had written to the company, thanking them for their gifts:

'It is very nice to think that we who are away on National Service are still in the minds of those left at Bournville,' wrote one employee serving with the RAF.

Another employee, with the RAMC, said, 'I can imagine the kindly spirit which exists behind the gifts and the unselfish giving of time and labour to make them possible.'

'It came at a very opportune moment as I had just been inoculated and as a result was confined to bed. I was cheered considerably to know that Bournville remembered us,' was the reply from someone in the RASC.

Another employee serving with the ATS was over the moon to receive the gifts. 'I am very much a smoker; I also have a sweet tooth; and the book is just the one I want to read. I feel deeply indebted to the "Sister Susie" for my lovely hand-knitted service scarf, and would like to compliment her on her good handiwork.'

But one employee was not so happy as although he enjoyed the four penny slabs of chocolate he was sent, especially during the night duty, he found the photograph of Bournville made him feel homesick. Another side-effect of serving had been him putting on a stone of weight. Unsurprising with all that gifted chocolate.

Some employees serving abroad wrote back to the company and described their experiences:

> *The scenery is very grand down here, but quaint villages are hardly entertaining during blackout hours … It's a long stretch from chocolate working to handling ammunition but it is surprising how one can adapt oneself to a new life, even a life of eternal TNT and brass buttons.* (Private L. Summers RAOC, who was in training in the West of England and had worked nights in the moulding department of the company.)

There were also plans to send parcels of chocolate and cocoa to the dependants of married men who were serving away as well as single people who had dependent parents.

Aside from gifting chocolate, they helped with the production of cretonne bags for use in French hospitals. The total amount needed was 15,000, with Bournville producing 100 and Birmingham in general pledging to make 1,000. Cretonne is a strong cotton- or flax-based material.

There were concerns that there had been a temporary shortage of supplies, but they were now confident they had enough wool to knit scarves and socks, etc, and this was increasing in capacity all the time. There was a big demand for knitted comforts as the depot wanted to send gifts to all those men serving away from home at Christmas. There were currently 1,000 men from the company serving, so this was proving to be a mammoth task. So much so, they were asking for more volunteers to help with the knitting as well as provide financial help. The cost of the 850lb of wool was estimated to be £340 (£20,382).

As well as supplying chocolate, cigarettes and other gifts, and making comforts for the armed forces, some employees also gave blood. The Blood Transfusion Service visited the factory, tested thirty women and enrolled them on the National Emergency Rota. It was hoped that more employees would come forward but acknowledged that many employees had already attended a similar drive at one of the main hospitals in the city.

When the National Savings Scheme came in, to help fund the war, Bournville held a campaign to encourage its employees to buy National Savings Certificates via their assisted purchasing scheme. They could be bought in instalments of up to sixty-five certificates at a time. The net cost of a new issue was £48 15s (£2,922) which they could pay monthly over two years. They started off very well with employees buying £155,000 (£9,291,826) from the start of the scheme to May 1940.

Great attention was given to the factory helping to beat the blackout by them hosting a home hobbies exhibition on 5 and 6 of December 1940, organised by the Men's Works Council and the Youths' Committee. The aim was to give people ideas on how to spend their time at home during the blackout that would help the war effort. It was suggested that people had forgotten how to amuse themselves and this forced-time at home would rekindle their creative abilities.

'Some say the blackout imprisons, but others say that it is one road to freedom,' was George Cadbury's opinion. It was time, he said for people to free themselves of being 'slaves' to entertainment by external means and give them the opportunity to 'realise our own possibilities'.

There were many exhibitors there including arts and crafts showing mechanical innovations, for instance, a road-making and excavating machine made of cocoa tins, the camera club, a gymnastics display, and shoe repairs. There was embroidery too, which was a nod to encouraging the working together of men and women in the home.

The company was also engaged in the education of its employees and was offering more evening classes as a response to the war-time restrictions and blackout. There was also a day school that would be housed in the dining block. They were slightly hampered by the wait for shelters to be installed.

The Bournville School of Arts and Crafts offered general design, craft and drawing tuition, with evening courses expected to begin at Bournville School from 8 January 1940, and at Selly Oak Technical Institute later that month.

The company took part in various sports throughout the war years too. They played football, bridge, hockey, rugby and table tennis, amongst other sports, and played against many teams including Birmingham University, Kidderminster and Smethwick. They also had a successful team of crown green bowlers, who won the championship shield of the Warwickshire and Worcestershire Junior League.

They even used sport to help with the fundraising. Bournville Sports was held to support the Lord Mayor of Birmingham's war relief fund. It involved a 10-mile cycle race for a silver trophy to be presented by the BSA company, as well as a 500-yard scratch-race and a mile flat race.

As the Dig for Victory campaign took hold, Bournville and Cadbury got involved too. By May 1940 there were 260 works allotments situated at Rowheath and Umberslade Road, with forty-two more now at Bournville. There were also plans for others at Hay Green Lane and Woodlands Park Road.

By 1942, Paul Cadbury made his annual statement at the Women's Council Annual Meeting, where the fact that they were a controlled industry was discussed. Industry was controlled by the government during the war, because they wanted to optimise efficiency. One of their measures was the Limitation of Supplies Order and the prioritisation of war manufacturing by way of ammunition and aircraft building, which later saw priorities changed to the allocation of resources with the formation of the Ministry of Production taking control.

For the company, this meant they were licensed to continue business but were under condition to become part of the Cocoa and Chocolate Wartime Association. Part of the condition of their membership was to set up their own committee and it appears that their hope was to pre-empt any restrictions and instructions forthcoming from the association and to try and have some say in what happened.

At the annual meeting, they went on to explain what happened, earlier

Savoy cabbages from the Rowheath plot, Bournville, 1940s. Courtesy of Cadbury Archive, Mondelez International.

on in the war, when raw materials were restricted and how they got around it. Normally a sales estimate is made on how much chocolate the company is likely to sell. This is then broken down into how much this equates to in the separate ingredients needed to make the chocolate products that the company buyers then go and purchase, often a bit more than required to allow sufficient margins. The ability to do this meant they could plan a few weeks to a few months ahead.

When the war started and raw materials, especially those from abroad, were running out due to the German Navy attacking and sinking merchant ships, they could no longer source and buy materials in the same way. The predecessor to the Wartime Association, the Manufacturing Confectioners' Alliance, had organised the sharing of depots and fair sharing of materials as previously discussed. But because there were further restrictions as the war went on, the company had to take more action involving the streamlining of their labour force. The workforce was smaller than usual as many men and women had either gone into the services or were volunteering for the war effort, which had been actively encouraged by the company. They were also deemed an essential industry for the war effort and had to walk the fine line of producing enough of their food product as well as having enough space in their factory for other essential war-work too:

> *I think that the most important, from the point of view of this business, and all of us, is that cocoa and chocolate is as an essential part of the food of the country at the present time. In a planned economy, there is so much meat, so much butter, margarine and so forth, and a block of chocolate every week is a very important part of our diet when the other things are in short supply.* (Paul Cadbury.)

In a country in the grip of rationing, a bar of chocolate, no matter how small, would have been a welcome treat. Paul Cadbury even went as far as stating that one of the reasons, according to the government, that Germany lost the Great War was, in part, due to their poor diet. He therefore vowed that the company would produce as many chocolate products as possible.

During the war, as in many other industries across Birmingham and the country, the company had to diversify. They were forced to abandon the production of their most popular Milk Tray assortments and milk chocolate bars because milk was needed elsewhere. Generally, however, the company, despite having to adapt, was positive:

It is no good putting our head in the sand like an ostrich ... hoping that something will turn up... We must be willing to face facts, and to retain our cheerfulness, whatever problems and difficulties beset us.

The road seems long and hard (for some it is very hard), but it is only by overcoming difficulties that we shall succeed, and it is by persevering that we shall survive.

Their perseverance paid off as they did survive, and today they are a multinational company and the second largest confectionary company in the world.

CHAPTER TEN

Crime

Most people were only too pleased to do their duty and help the war effort but, as always, whenever there is war or conflict there will be those who will either try and capitalise on the sudden opportunities that rationing and war present or use the blackout to their criminal advantage.

One particular crime highlighted in the *Birmingham Mail* was a flurry of women shoplifters. One of these women was a mother of five children, who had, due to a previous theft of money, already been bound over. She even got her 13-year-old daughter involved, resulting in her daughter receiving a sentence of twelve months' probation and herself one month in prison.

In another case, two local men were charged with 'attempting to obtain 3d (75p) by false pretences'. It involved Henry Evans of Camden Street, Birmingham, aged 47, and James Morton of Adelaide Street, Birmingham, aged 54, who had been trying to sell, by trickery, torch batteries that were not the strength they were advertised to be.

They had rigged up a bulb in the High Street to a higher strength battery, which was hidden from view, and pretended that the lower strength batteries were the higher strength ones instead. Although they pleaded not guilty, there had been several witnesses who had crowded round the table. The prosecution described the actions of both men as a 'very mean and despicable fraud by both men trying to make money out of the blackout conditions'.

Conscientious objectors could find themselves not only pariahs in their own communities but also in trouble with the law. One such incident was reported in the *Birmingham Mail* on 6 January 1940. Under the headline 'He Won't Take the Blame', it was said that at a tribunal in London a man claiming to be a conscientious objector, in his defence of not wishing to fight, had said:

Supermen invented the aeroplane. It is not my fault that the ape has got hold of it.

Another conscientious objector had the opinion that the Finnish people should have just let the Russians 'march in' and not co-operated with them. Mr Brister from Kings Heath was keen to point out that he thought war was 'against humanity', and the current situation could have been settled by more peaceful means. The judge granted him an exemption so long as he carried on working at the chocolate factory.

Mr Chambers from Kings Norton was also against the principle of war, claiming it not to be right for some people. He felt that because the Royal Army Medical Corps (RAMC) was part of the 'war machine' that even that was out of bounds to him because it was still part of the army. The judge replied with:

Well you have got to be under the control of something.

Mr Chambers conceded that he would assist the Red Cross but not help those wounded men in the field. The judge duly registered him for non-combatant work.

There was a distinction made between pacifists and conscientious objectors. Mr Cheadle, a Christian Scientist, was not in agreement with war but was aware that Christian Scientists were not pacifists. 'If there was more love in the world, there would be no need for war,' he proclaimed. Although the judge was sympathetic to Mr Cheadle's words, he still took his name off the register, to which Mr Cheadle vowed to appeal.

It wasn't just one faith that objected to war and its members finding themselves at a tribunal. Tribunals were special courts set up to hear applications from those seeking to avoid exemptions from having to fight or take on other non-combatant roles. A tailor from Kings Heath, Mr Cohen was of the Jewish faith and said:

Almighty God has taught me not to take the sword in one hand and religion in the other.

The judge refused his application for exemption, so Mr Cohen was going to appeal and told the tribunal that he wouldn't pick up any guns that were offered to him.

Another local man, Mr Cole from Edgbaston, worked for the Birmingham Corporation and claimed to be not 100 per cent pacifist but was adamant that should the corporation come under the control of the armed forces he would be forced to resign. Part of the condition for his continued exemption was that he continued to work for the corporation.

It wasn't just those with a trade, like tailors and council workers, who were heard at tribunals. A school teacher, Mr Condry from Harborne, also didn't support the war, purely from an ethical standpoint. He had read history and come to the conclusion that no war could ever be called 'just'. He did not feel that war was 'morally justifiable', and declined to help protect his country. He was granted exemption.

The judge was, at times, exasperated, by some of the excuses behind some men's objections to war. A Mr Cork from Cato Street would not work with the RAMC because he objected to 'patching up men to fight again'. The judge stated that he'd heard that 'silly' story and was fed up with it. He explained that the RAMC was to help injured men to get fit again, but not necessarily fit to fight but for life. He stated that Mr Cork's view and that of others like him were 'not fair to your fellow men'. As Mr Cork worked making munitions he was granted exemption.

In January 1940, Sir John Anderson had a warning for those against war such as pacifists and conscientious objectors. Sir John had joined the Colonial Office in 1905. He took up the post of joint undersecretary in Ireland, and was part of the committee dealing with the general strike before being appointed governor of Bengal in 1932.

On his return to Britain in 1938, he was elected to the House of Commons and was put in charge of the ARP. It was in this role that he said the country would end the 'Nazi rule of jungle war', and urged the population to be on their guard against 'pacifist propaganda', which he said could be 'subtle' and at its foundations 'at least suspect'.

He was also fearful that the expected widespread attacks on Britain that the towns and cities across the country had been preparing for had not happened. This was no time for complacency or for dropping their guard. He was particularly concerned about parents bringing their evacuated children back home when, although it was relatively quiet, the danger was still present.

He posed a question for the pacifists: 'Are we to live under the rule of law or the rule of brute force?'

In defence of conscientious objectors and his church, one Christadelphian, Mr Warre, said, 'We are not here to make objectors.' He was speaking at the Midland Tribunal for Conscientious Objectors held in Birmingham on 10 January 1940. He was there to support one of his church's members, Mr Skeates, from Erdington, who had formerly been a Baptist but felt that the Christadelphians better suited his opinions on war and so switched when he had a discussion about pacifism with a Christadelphian eighteen months previously.

Mr Skeates was a worker at an aerodrome but had handed in his notice when he came to think of his feelings about war and the work he was doing to help the war effort. He now worked in a hospital as a porter. Mr Skeates, much to his and Mr Warre's relief, was allowed to stay, conditionally, on the register.

The judge wasn't so understanding of Mr Sharpe from Hall Green, who claimed he'd been a pacifist from five years of age. The judge, amongst much laughter in the court, replied: 'I suppose if your father used force to you, you did not offer any resistance.'

Mr Sharpe was finding it difficult to find employment as most of the suitable firms were now doing war-work, which was against his beliefs. He was an instrument-maker. He was given a two-month adjournment, time for him to seek out employment that was both of national importance and sat easy with his conscience.

Another adjournment was made in a case where a father represented his son. The son, a brewer's drayman from Aston, said little with his father doing the majority of the talking. The son had some hearing difficulties and couldn't get across his thoughts, but his father said he was against killing on account of what previous wars had done to his family. He came from a military family.

In order to appease the judge, he was keen to tell him that there were strict guidelines and tests to be passed before someone could join the Christadelphian Church, and denied that his church could be a 'hiding place' for those wishing to get out of fighting in the war.

People were not brought before the courts just to test their convictions for peace or because they had stolen something, they also found themselves in breach of the many, and often changing, regulations and restrictions impinged upon them throughout the war years.

One notable violation was the number of motorists who were caught out under the Lighting Restrictions Order, particularly, for some reason, in Solihull. Some motorists had been observed driving their vehicles at night with lamps that exceeded 7 watts and also neglecting to have hoods fitted to lamps so that light would not be emitted above eye level/greater than 25 feet, and potentially gain the unwelcome attention of enemy aircraft.

One such motorist, Mr Robinson from Radbourne Road, Shirley, had written a letter to the court, questioning the police's ability to accurately gauge the wattage of his bulbs. The police said they could see markings inside the bulb that indicated its wattage. This particular case was adjourned so that Mr Robinson could attend the court. Similar cases were fined 10s (£30) each.

With the blackout restrictions came the risk of more accidents on the roads, due to reduced visibility, with pedestrians and cyclists most at risk. One case was heard in Birmingham County Court and presided over by Judge D.L. Finnemore. Mr Turvey of Acocks Green had been knocked over by a car when he was cycling along Warwick Road on 4 September 1939. He accused Mr Clarke of Moseley of being the driver.

It was ascertained that Mr Turvey was cycling on the correct side of the road at a distance of around 3 feet from the kerb. But, even though a requirement under the Lighting Restrictions Order that cyclists should have a rear red light came into force on 1 September, Mr Turvey had not complied. Mr Clarke confirmed that he had not seen Mr Turvey or his cycle before he hit him.

The judge ruled that Mr Turvey had been negligent for the absence of the red rear light, and Mr Clarke was not as he was driving under blackout conditions. If Mr Turvey had the required red light, the accident could have been avoided. In mitigation, Mr Turvey stated that he had not known about the new requirement for cyclists until after the accident, blaming the odd hours that he worked. It was agreed by both Mr Turvey and Mr Clarke that they had seen lots of cyclists around without red lights.

The judge said that ignorance was not an excuse and everyone needed to keep up with the rules and abide by them as soon as they came into force. He was equally dismissive of Mr Clarke's excuses, stating that had Mr Clarke been paying attention and driving appropriately, he would have seen Mr Turvey. Even in blackout conditions the driver should have been able to see the painted kerbs and, given the fine weather at the time, would have had visibility ahead of at least 3 yards. Mr Turvey did have a reflector on the rear of his bike and the appropriate regulation white end on the rear mudguard. Mr Clarke was ordered to pay £20 (£1,198) damages to Mr Turvey.

Even an ex-policeman found himself being fined £1 10s (£89) as well as costs of £1 11s (£92) in a court in Droitwich. Mr Crump, aged 27, who was now a corporal in the army, had been accused of careless driving and without a licence on the Worcester to Birmingham Road. He caused mayhem when he swerved on to the wrong side of the road and hit a lorry, which itself had to swerve and, unfortunately, hit a cyclist.

So concerned were the Ministry of War Transport about the issue of transport and the blackout, that they issued warnings in the newspapers. The *Birmingham Mail* carried them in their pages. One advert said 'Your Turn May Come Tonight', and warned walkers of the 'danger of the dark'. It stated that thousands had already been killed on the roads and that pedestrians carried their lives on their legs. They were urged to be careful and mindful of car drivers who may not be able to see them clearly.

Attention was also drawn to drivers, warning them that pedestrians were vulnerable in the blackout and to drive slowly.

It wasn't just light that caused problems. It was noise too. Under the fantastic headline 'Birmingham Fines First Siren-Tooter', one paper urged its readers to refrain from making any noise that could be mistaken for an air-raid siren.

Alfred Sargent, from Northfield, was trying to fix the horn on his motorbike and, in order to see if he had been successful, he'd sounded it several times. Unluckily for him one of his neighbours was a special constable and had been woken up by the noise, believing it to be an air-raid siren. Other neighbours thought so too.

The Control of Noise (Defence) Order No. 2, 1939 saw Alfred fined 10s, (£30) with 14s 6d (£43) costs at Birmingham Police Court, even though he thought the matter was 'trivial'.

The country was at war. Many people were going above and beyond the call of duty, putting themselves out and suffering hardship, denying themselves some of the home comforts they were used to. Children were separated from their parents and sent many miles away to live, albeit temporarily, with strangers. The city was busy preparing itself for whatever horrors the *Luftwaffe* were about to unleash upon them. But that didn't deter a gang of local thieves.

The Birmingham Stipendiary jailed eight local men who had received stolen sandbags. It came to light that across the whole city some 50,000 government-issue sandbags had been stolen from their official stores. They were worth an estimated £1,000 (£61,700). These sandbags had been distributed for the protection of some of the city's buildings and inhabitants. There had been some difficulty finding out how they were stolen, but they had gone. Of the eight men, the majority were known metal thieves.

They came from Newham Hill, Kingstanding, Tenby Street, Moreton Street, Well Street, Albion Street and Lower Town Street, and received between three and twelve months hard labour each for their crime. The judge stated that they had all of them played a part in a 'widespread conspiracy'.

This gang were not the only ones pilfering the supply of sandbags. It was a popular and lucrative crime, with the government having supplied the city with 8,500,000 sandbags, worth £100,000 (£6,170,000).

One of the men had spoken to a local estate agent who, in good faith, purchased 3,000 of the stolen bags. This particular gang-member was the man who did most of the contacting of potential buyers. It is interesting to note that of the eight accused, seven of them had changed their names but all of them had had their collars felt by the law before. The ringleader had been home on sick leave from the Royal Army Service Corps (RASC) but this was his thirtieth appearance in court. Another of the gang was not far behind, on his twenty-eighth appearance and, at the time of the crime, a serving member of the Royal Artillery, but was on a licence from a Borstal institution.

Another theft in January 1940, this time the list included eleven pairs of anti-gas eye shields, an electric razor and £2-worth (£119) of chocolate, was heard in Birmingham Juvenile Court. The items, amongst other things, were, perhaps shockingly, lifted by three children aged between 11 and 12, taken from cars. All three children received punishments – the 11-year-old and one of the 12-year-olds were put on probation, with the other 12-year-old sent to an approved school.

Soldiers and ex-soldiers were turning to crime. A private in the Royal Army Ordnance Corps (RAOC) was alleged to have stolen £65 (£3,896) and three gold rings from a woman he'd been living with for seven months. The woman said there had been an argument and that the man had hit her. Although the man admitted he'd 'touched' some of her money, it wasn't as much as the amount she claimed. He also said that another man had been in the house and he was assaulted by that other man and so had left because he was afraid.

He claimed he'd gone to London and then on to Hampshire to see the wife he hadn't seen for seventeen years. He said he only took £15 (£899) of the woman's money because she had given it to him, but due to them both being 'hopelessly' drunk, she couldn't remember that. He was given two months' hard labour.

Other thefts at the time (January 1940), reported in the *Birmingham Mail*, included an 18-year-old man from Smethwick who stole 4s 9d-worth (£14) of confectionery. He was jailed for two months with a 15-year-old, his accomplice, and fined £2 (£119)

Even a person's workplace wasn't exempt from thieving hands. One man, a 26-year-old labourer living in Aston Road, pleaded guilty at Birmingham Police Court to stealing 3d (75p) from the pocket of another employee at the Delta Metal Company in Dartmoor Street.

The company had had a few thefts reported by its employees and decided to set a trap. They deliberately placed three marked pennies into a coat pocket and the defendant was seen taking the money. He'd been caught red-handed, but said he hadn't stolen anything before. He was fined 20s (£59).

Professional people and those regarded as pillars of the community were also turning to crime. Mr Ridgeway, aged 24, was a qualified pharmaceutical chemist, who was charged with supplying a noxious substance for illegal purposes and for conspiring with two people to do the same thing. He was paid 30s (£89) for the substances that were worth about 3s (£8). He pleaded guilty and was bound over for three years.

With war comes tragedy. The death of many men in the fields, air space and seas of war, the killing of hundreds of civilians at home from air-raids, but, just as accidents happen in peacetime, they also occur in wartime. One particularly sad case involved the finding of the body of an amateur racing cyclist in January 1940. Mr Hughes, aged 25, from Washwood Heath, was found dead, still astride his bicycle on a road near to Woodlands Farm, Bacon's End. How he came to die was not known. He had been riding on the correct side of the road but had suffered a fractured skull and abrasions to his left thigh.

A pedestrian was found dead in the road at Hockley Heath on 31 December 1939 at 12.40am. Mr Walton, a 39-year-old aircraftman from Hunton Heath, was found by a chauffeur who claimed he had not run him over. Death was caused by shock, internal bleeding and many fractures to his spine, but the car that hit him was not traced.

Another tragic accidental death occurred at the Austin Aero Company factory. Mr Garner, aged 35, from West Heath, had been working for a contractor to help paint camouflage on the outside of the factory, but he fell 20 feet through an open trapdoor. Mr Seal, an engineer with the factory, said the walkway with the trapdoor was used by 100 men each day and so it had not been possible to have that door shut. Another worker giving evidence said he had been walking in front of Mr Garner, but Garner had not stepped over the door and had fallen.

Another inquest in Birmingham heard the tragic case of the death of a tram driver. Cyril Hinett, aged 60, of Franklin Road, Kings Norton, was an auxiliary driver for City Transport and fell from the tram platform. One of the passengers and a witness to the fall was James Brewer from Quarry Lane, who described how the tram was making its way along Bristol Street South, towards Rednal, at 7.30pm in August 1945. Unfortunately, as they approached Bodenham Road the driver stuck his hand out and then fell whilst another tram passed.

James managed to get to the controls and stop the tram, even though he had no idea what he was doing. He dashed back to where Mr Hinett had fallen. Harry Parker, of Lockwood Road, Northfield, who had been driving the passing tram, immediately applied the emergency brakes of his tram, but in the heat of the moment couldn't be sure if he had hit the deceased or not. In the event traces of blood were found on the front of the tram. Mr Hinett died in hospital on 30 August 1945 and the verdict was accidental death.

There was an interesting case that came before the courts in September 1945. There were accusations that a soldier from Birmingham had worn an SS uniform and offered Heil Hitler salutes whilst on parade. It had occurred when the defendant and witnesses had been interned at a German prisoner-of-war camp. The SS, or *Schutzstaffel*, which translates to Protection Squadron, were under the auspices of the National Socialist German Workers' Party and Hitler.

At the resulting court martial held at Farnborough for Edward Martin (26) of the Essex Scottish Regiment in the Canadian Army, one of those men who witnessed the behaviour, Private L.T. Freeman of No.7 Commandos, stated that four men, alongside Martin and himself, had been given the SS uniforms when they were at Hildersheim, a propaganda school in Germany.

He described the uniforms as having a Union Jack around the right arm of the uniform, with the left sporting the Free Corps flash. They were also issued with pistols and caps that had the death's head symbol on it.

The charge against Martin was aiding the enemy while acting as an informer and voluntarily acting as a member of an organisation controlled by the enemy, by the name of the British Free Corps. Martin pled not guilty to all charges, claiming he had been working with the Germans to get information from them to help the British cause.

The corps, previously known as the British Legion of St George, was organised by the Nazis who had become aware of John Amery, the son of Leo Amery who was at one time the Minister for India under Churchill. His view that the Jews and Soviets were planning to overthrow the west resonated with Nazi Germany and Amery was asked to visit Berlin, which he did. Having the son of a British minister was a gift to the German propaganda machine.

By 1943, Amery began his recruitment drive in Paris to build a 1,500-strong group of prisoners-of-war. But Amery was way off the mark. If he was counting on support from the prisoners-of-war, he was to be disappointed, as he only managed to gain one supporter there, the rest of the men taking umbrage at this affront to the British campaign. Eventually he gained more recruits. At the end of the war, as one of the corps' members, Martin, found out, those men involved were arrested and Amery himself was hanged for treason in 1945.

One of the witnesses, Freeman, stated that the only conditions to them joining the corps were that they would remain with the corps until the war ended and that they had no Jewish blood. Martin, on the other hand, said he only changed tack with the German officers when they became suspicious of his motives.

Having met Martin at a prisoner-of-war camp in 1943, witness Private A.H. Pagett of the 7th Battalion, Worcestershire Regiment, said he had even changed his name to Nicholson. He explained how they used to have a radio hidden under the bed. They'd managed to hide it from the guards for a year until Martin arrived. Martin was told he was welcome to listen to it as long as he didn't tell anyone about it.

When Martin was led away by a German officer from the camp after saying he was ill, it was felt that it was no coincidence when the camp had to parade and while they were gone the radio disappeared.

At another camp, Stalag 8B, Lansdorff, another witness, Gunner T. Joyce of the Royal Engineers, Kings Lynn, said he had seen Martin dressed in the SS uniform. He allegedly confessed that he was working with the Germans, but 'not doing big stuff'.

As the court martial progressed, Martin claimed he had been trying to mislead the Germans and was adamant that he hadn't informed the guards about the hidden radio. He even went as far as claiming that he was moved to that camp as a test to see if he was really working for the Germans or double-crossing them. Then he tried to implicate three other prisoners-of-war. When he arrived at Luckenwalde Camp in July 1943, he met three prisoners who, he stated, he was suspicious about because he'd seen them passing notes to each other and to the Germans, which led him to believe they were 'informers'. They were Private J. Welch, Private Gallaher and Stoker Rose.

Martin also claimed, when asked why he had joined the corps, that he had done so to 'get a kick back at Jerry'.

It wasn't just some prisoners-of-war finding themselves in hot water. One Birmingham man, Terence Egan, aged 24, found himself in front of the city's magistrates, charged, in 1945, with obtaining £3 (£179) by false pretences and stealing two clothing coupon books.

He worked at the time for Birmingham Hospitals Contributory Association as an ambulance orderly. One day a man, whose wife had died and Egan had previously taken to hospital, was unable to locate his clothing ration books, which he needed to buy a suit. Egan offered to get the man a suit for £3 (£179), which he took, but having been paid, he did not get a suit.

This wasn't the only incidence. Egan also told a few more people he'd met in the course of his job that their old ration books had been found back at the hospital and if they handed over their new books to him he could get their old ones back to them. Pleading guilty, Egan received a nine-month prison sentence and confessed to a further three more coupon book thefts.

There were many laws and orders passed throughout the war that would often catch the seemingly innocent and ignorant off-guard. One woman found herself on the wrong end of the food restrictions in 1945. Mrs Elsie Mellers, who managed a confectionery business in Alum Rock Road, was fined £5 (£203) for producing jellies without the relevant licence in 1945.

The jellies, which were found to contain 80 per cent water, gelatine and colouring, with one containing strawberry essence, were on sale for 9d (£1) each at an undisclosed Birmingham shop. Over the previous four months, her business had sold 5,169 of these jellies and made £1,069 (£43,500) Pleading not guilty, the woman explained that the jellies were not sold as food and customers were able to flavour the jellies after they had been bought.

Another duo from the city, R. Hawkins, aged 35, and E. Smith, aged 32, brothers-in-law from Kings Norton, found themselves charged with breaking-and-entering a bake-house and assaulting a policeman in the process on the night of 26 August 1945.

PC Brown said he had noticed a light on at the bake-house and when he investigated he found the two men inside, who tried to get out. Unfortunately, in the ensuing scuffle, PC Brown received a punch to his eye from Smith that needed hospital treatment.

Whether you were in the forces, a tradesperson or businessperson, trying to get out of active service or just going about your daily business, if you put a foot wrong and were seen to not be doing your patriotic duty, you were likely to find yourself in hot water. But not everyone had crime on their mind. Just as the war brought opportunities to bring out the worst in people, it also brought out the good and the people of Birmingham had their charitable side too.

CHAPTER ELEVEN

Charity

Wars are expensive and although the government provided some relief it was up to the people of Birmingham and the council to take up the challenge and plough their efforts into assisting the government by fundraising.

One of the areas in which such relief would be invaluable was the provision of relief centres in the aftermath of any bombing. The superintendent relieving officer, W.B. Whitton, stated that those who found themselves homeless due to bombing should seek support and direction from local police and other officials to one of the twenty-three relief stations across the city.

Each centre would be well-equipped with cooking facilities, rations and heating, blankets, bedding and clothing, which had been provided through the Lady Mayoress's Depot. The centres could sleep 4,000 people with a further forty overflow stations having room for 6,500 more. Various churches and organisations across the city volunteered their halls and other accommodation to help.

The main stations were situated in places such as 78 Cornwall Street, 94 Alcester Street Methodist School, the Baptist School in Alexander Road, Acocks Green, Nechells Hall on Nechells Park Road, the Community Hall in Kingstanding, and Union Row Congregational School in Grove Lane. The Citizen's Society also offered their assistance in association with the lord mayor's fund designed to help the homeless and destitute in the city.

National Savings Certificates were popular. Since the kiosk that sold them and Defence Bonds had opened in front of the Council House in January 1940, 1,656 certificates and bonds had been sold, valued at £1,010 (£60,546).

There was no shortage of advice for the people of Birmingham when it came to War Savings Certificates and Defence Bonds, and the *Birmingham Mail* often carried adverts informing readers of the options available to them. In 1940, the certificates were priced at 15s (£44) each with a value of 17s (£50) after five years and 20s 6d (£61) after ten. You could buy the Defence Bonds at £5 (£299) each in multiples of £5 (£299). People could also go to the Post Office Savings Bank and the Trustee Savings Bank to deposit any amount between 1s (£3) and a cap of £500 (£29,973) annually, according to the National Savings Committee whose slogan on this particular advert was 'Lend to defend the right to be free'.

Employers were advised to set up their own National Savings Group for their employees as well.

The lord mayor and lady mayoress were no strangers to leading the charity drive during the war. The lady mayoress had a depot at 75 Broad Street in the city, which was used as a clearing house for the Lord Mayor of Birmingham's war relief fund. Over Christmas 1939, the depot dispatched many comforts to those men from Birmingham serving in the forces. They included 570lb of plum pudding, 58,000 cigarettes, 1,650 woollen mittens, and forty handkerchiefs to the British Expeditionary Force.

For the troops at home they sent 8,191lb of plum pudding, 7,410 cigarettes, 3,277 woollen comforts, and 251 blankets. The Royal Navy received twenty-seven blankets, 134lb of sweets, seventy tins of biscuits and, interestingly, one ukulele.

Other items, such as games, books, shaving soap and musical instruments, were sent on to the Lord-Lieutenant of Warwickshire's fund. As well as items for the forces, civilians were also catered for. There were 920 parcels made up for evacuees with eighty babies' vests and twenty suits sent to Finland. Those who had suffered in the air-raids were sent 1,200 garments, of which 126 were complete outfits. The main depot also had thirty-eight sub-depots and 142 working parties working hard to make supplies for the hospitals. They had been given 4,000 yards of free material to make 213 shirts for those refugees from Poland, with nine bales of hospital supplies being sent to Finland. They'd also had to order in more wool to help cope with the demand. It was charity production to a massive scale.

In January 1940, the working party of the Hall Green Unionist's Association were called on by Sir Patrick Hannon, MP for Moseley. He saw, first-hand, the effort and hours being put into producing comforts for the forces and at home. He believed that Great Britain would be victorious in this war and that the 'support' and 'common sense' of the world would see to it that they did.

Whilst he was there, he appealed to the women of Birmingham to do all they could to raise the profile of savings certificates and war bonds by using their 'opportunities as propagandists'.

Earlier in the day he had visited the BSA factory, where he witnessed 'great enthusiasm' from the workforce to purchase certificates and bonds. He was pleased that over 2 million women across Great Britain had already volunteered to help with the war effort. As a bit of an incentive, he threw in a competition for the women of Hall Green, offering a prize of £10 (£599) to the person who managed to get the most subscribers to the War Savings Fund.

They also held dances and other events to help boost funds. One example was a carnival dance to be held at the Palaise De Danse in Monument Road on Friday 26 January 1940, from 7pm – 12 midnight, costing 1/6 per ticket. It boasted two bands and was billed as 'You will be helping the Tommies'.

Of course, with the start of the Second World War and with memories of the First World War still relatively fresh in people's minds, another charity that was around, as it very much still is today, was the poppy appeal. Many people's grandparents and parents fought in the First World War, or had been involved in war-work at home, or remembered what it was like on the Home Front at the time, so the poppy appeal was much respected. The 1939 Birmingham poppy appeal was pleased to have raised £10,428 16s 0d (£625,178) in street collections, £2,407 6s 8d (£144,313) in works' collections and a further £446 1s 9d (£26,741) in donations and sundries.

There was also an appeal for the people of Birmingham to help with the Lord Mayor of Birmingham's War Fund Emblem Day, which was being held to send comforts to Birmingham men in the forces and their dependants left at home, as well as helping the general war effort.

Just as they needed volunteers for ARP work and first aid, amongst other things, they also needed street collectors for

Saturday 27 January, to collect donated money, as well as district organisers for areas such as Kings Heath, Sparkbrook and Selly Oak. Interested volunteers were to attend the Emblem Day Headquarters at 9 Easy Row.

Sporting events helped raise much-needed money for the war and to relieve suffering. In one instance in 1940, the Midland Golfers' Association appointed a special committee to help organise a series of competitions of which the proceeds would go to war charities. They agreed to hold a meeting on 22 February, with a four-ball event to be played over eighteen holes. Another competition would be held later in March 1940 at Moor Hall Golf Course. The competition previously held in 1939 at Little Aston resulted in £80 (£313,109) being given to the Lord Mayor of Birmingham's Red Cross fund.

Boxing in Birmingham did a lot for war charities. There had been a draw at the Rose and Crown Hotel, Bromsgrove Street, for a charity amateur boxing tournament, of which the proceeds, similarly to the golfing competitions, would be going towards the Lord Mayor of Birmingham's war relief fund. Each match was to have six competitors and involve three rounds with three four-round junior matches. The whole tournament would be overseen by the Austin Club. The lord mayor wrote to the organisers, thanking them.

Competing from the north of the city would be Morris Commercial v Aston and Wolseley v John Wright's. The south would see Austin v Bournbrook and Chamberlain & Hookhams v Imperial.

Due to the tyranny of Hitler and his troops, there were also many displaced refugees that found themselves receiving Birmingham hospitality. There was a special New Year's party for the refugees held in early January 1940 at the Islington Methodist Institute at Five Ways. Refugees from Czechoslovakia, Germany and Austria attended.

Birmingham people, in the war years, were a charitable lot and their contribution to help those in need, including servicemen and refugees, was immense. What makes their charitable efforts all the more amazing is the fact that they were donating money, items and making comforts at a time when they themselves were feeling the pinch of restriction and financial loss.

CHAPTER TWELVE

The Role of the Hospitals

Birmingham was fortunate to have many fine hospitals within its boundaries that were at the forefront of medical research, and some that were considered to be centres of excellence. The Second World War was a period of change for Birmingham. Medical advances were occurring, but hospitals were under pressure from those residents requiring not only normal everyday health care and surgery, but also those needing help following injuries from the heavy bombardments the city had to endure. They were also at risk of being bombed themselves.

The Royal Orthopaedic Hospital was situated on Bristol Road South. The building itself was erected in 1766, with extensions built in 1791. From its early humble beginnings, it provided care and treatment for many patients who would have not survived or would have lived a grim life had the hospital, its facilities and staff not been there. The area it served, according to the Population Act return of 1801, showed 12,044 houses were lived in with a total of 60,822 residents. When outlying areas such as Deritend and Bordesley were taken in to account, this figure jumped to 69,384.

In 1794, there were 325 patients who had been seen at home by hospital staff, of which 246 were sick. Their midwifery staff had seen forty-eight cases, and thirty-one patients received vaccinations. By December 1866, the number of patients seen at the hospital was 7,100, with 1,169 vaccinations given. For an idea of how valuable the hospital was to the community of Birmingham, from 1793 to 1866 there had been 328,312 patients, 36,035 were midwifery-related, with 196,834 sick patients and 95,413 vaccinations.

The original hospital did not specialise in orthopaedics until 1877, when thoughts turned to the better care of those who were physically disabled, with the commencement of the General Institute for the Relief of Bodily Deformities in that year.

Most of the local hospitals at the time were run on a subscription basis, where people could buy tickets to either use the facilities or nominate them for someone else, and this was no different for the newly formed orthopaedic hospital. Things were not exactly fine, however. The town had its deprived areas and there was not a lot of wealth to go around. Uptake of subscriptions and donations to the existing hospitals had been low, and this was the problem the orthopaedic hospital also faced. People lived in unfit, squalid conditions and many needed treatment. Their need and the pressures on the hospital's facilities could only increase, due to the population rising from 70,000 in 1801 to 90,000 in 1817.

The remit of the hospital was now to focus on complaints such as hernias, as well as obtaining equipment and expertise that would help them relieve the suffering and improve the lives of those afflicted by physical deformity. Suggested subscription fees included: 1 guinea would help two patients for rupture; 2 guineas for four patients for rupture; and one patient for bodily deformity.

As early as 1937, the hospital received enquiries from the Ministry of Health about provisions and accommodation the hospital could supply in the event of a national emergency. The hospital had recently acquired a mobile shock-proof X-Ray machine that could be transported to the wards, and they had requested £2,592 (£40,000) for the building of extensions. A year later, the crisis and possibility of war was deepening and contingency plans were drawn up by the hospital, including evacuation. The Dower House in Lapworth, 6 miles from Solihull, owned by Colonel and Mrs J.L. Mellor, had said that part of the house could be used as an auxiliary hospital. Another family, the Williamses of Weatheroak Hall, Kings Norton, were happy to have part of their house adapted to care for some of the hospital's child patients.

It wasn't long before the hospital's plans were put to the test when they had to evacuate forty-two children from the Woodlands to the Forelands, with twenty more children indeed going to the Dower House at Lapworth. This was because part of the house had become a Voluntary Aid Detachment Hospital. These were large houses or manor houses that had had some of their rooms lent to the military to act as convalescence hospitals for servicemen.

Wards 8 and 9 under construction, 1939. Courtesy of The Royal Orthopaedic Hospital NHS Trust, Birmingham.

Despite the war now being in full swing, the hospital saw, through many of its planned extensions and alterations including at the Woodlands, a new X-Ray department and the massage department, with a new ward block becoming functional in May 1940. However, the hospital did not emerge out of the war unscathed, with reports of damage from the bombing in the autumn of 1940.

Hospitals, a place of safety and somewhere to be treated, were not immune to the horror of war. There was one particular incident that shook the staff and local community, which the then Matron Fanny Smith wrote about in her report book:

23rd November, 1940. Enemy Action.

At 1.45 a.m. a high explosive bomb hit the corner of the Administrative Block – damaging four wards, Miss Moiet's bedroom (Nurse Steinhausen and Nurse Ponder) The Teacher's Room and Mattress Room, which were demolished. The bomb came through the roof and two

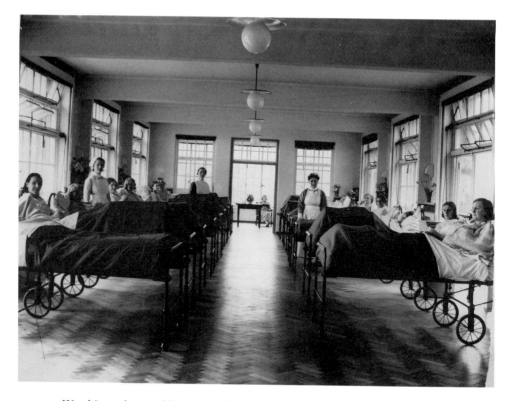

Ward 9, in the new block, Woodland's Hospital, 1940. Courtesy of The Royal Orthopaedic Hospital, Birmingham, NHS Trust.

> *bedrooms, to the Teacher's Room where Sister Galloway and Sister Daniels were having their night meal … They were found under the debris of the Mattress Room four hours later.*
>
> *A second bomb fell on the corner of the New Block and exploded near the bathroom. Most of the windows of the service block and side wards were blown out, and also some of the doors, and part of the Sheffield Covered Way. The patients who were in the side ward were not hurt, but one man had a slight cut on the forehead, and the beds were covered with glass. The patients were wonderfully brave, so many were helpless but none complained. The sisters and nurses worked hard to move the patients under cover of another ward. The cooks made tea for everyone. The co-operation and help from everyone was marvellous.*

Another high explosive fell among the trees, and it was thought to be unexploded, so four wards were evacuated next morning ... One incendiary bomb fell between the Nurses Home and the Rabone Hall and was immediately extinguished by Sister Hyden ... the rest of the nurses and maids were not told of the tragic circumstances until they were called the next morning.

... the telephone girls were very brave, they were in darkness and water was pouring down from the fractured pipes. The electric light was off for the remainder of the night but was connected the next day. The Telephone and Exchanges were off until the 27th but one private line was intact ...

The gas was off for 8 days, the water for 9 days, the corporation brought tanks and the well was used by pumping, the water was pumped out for sanitary arrangements. Drinking water was fetched twice daily from Middlepark Road by Mrs. Burton, from Barnt Green, who came daily and drove our lorry. The water and milk had to be boiled. The heating was off 10 days.

Despite the damage and threat from further air-raids, the hospital carried on as best it could. There were patients who needed care and treatment and nothing could be allowed to get in the way of that.

Matron Fanny Smith also said that the two nurses who were killed in the incident, Sister Galloway, who hailed from Glasgow and was the night superintendent, and Sister Daniels from Streetly, who was the relief night sister. They had both joined the staff on 1 May 1936. Matron led a tribute to them extolling their virtue and the work they did for the patients. There is a plaque on the wall inside the hospital commemorating their passing.

On 24 January 1944, a ceremony took place at the Woodlands where the memorial plaque was unveiled by Dame Elizabeth Cadbury for Sister Galloway and Sister Daniels and all the staff who faced danger. The dedication pointed out that they had done their duty in a situation of grave danger and 'thought not of their own safety, but only of the welfare of the patients there'.

The war was not only affecting Great Britain, and this thought was reflected in the further actions of the hospital when they

The plaque. Courtesy of The Royal Orthopaedic Hospital, Birmingham, NHS Trust.

welcomed Belgian patients to their wards in the Woodlands. Because the Ministry of Health was keen to help, they asked the hospital to take in patients from Belgium. The hospital was honoured to be of service and forty civilian orthopaedic patients (twenty-four women and sixteen men) were admitted, along with their Belgian matron (Matron de Wolfe), three nurses and one of the patient's wives. They had been in a hospital in Ostend when the Germans invaded. Due to her work with the Belgian patients, Matron Fanny Smith was awarded a special commendation by the Belgian government.

With the bomb damage and more patients requiring care, the committee were keen to increase their income to help pay for increased costs. They sent out an appeal to their subscribers, showing them how to make £1 (£43) become £2 (£83) by signing a Deed of Covenant that would enable them to pay their subscription for seven years while the income tax rate meant the subscription would effectively be doubled.

In the same year, the committee reported that the Woodlands had a bed complement of 244, with eighteen beds for private patients, while the Forelands, Bromsgrove, had seventy-four beds.

The last fete before the war. Releasing balloons, 1939. Courtesy of The Royal Orthopaedic Hospital, Birmingham, NHS Trust.

Matron Fanny Smith (centre) with a group of nurses at the hospital. Courtesy of The Royal Orthopaedic Hospital, Birmingham, NHS Trust.

Belgian patients on ward during the war. Courtesy of The Royal Orthopaedic Hospital, Birmingham, NHS Trust.

In 1943, there was a steady rise in workload, but many planned building works were postponed due to the war. The hospital witnessed their expenditure top £4,321 (£100,000). They optimistically looked forward to the end of the war with the setting up of a Post-War Development Committee, with another operating theatre in the pipeline that would further bolster the hospital's reputation as the main centre for excellence in the field of orthopaedics in the Midlands.

Because concerns amongst the committee were raised about the suitability of the premises in Broad Street, they were going to have to make some decisions about how they operated from the different sites as the Broad Street site was not suitable for extension. There were rumours that the state was about to form a medical service – what we now know as the National Health Service – and they wanted to be ready for this but felt it impossible to make changes until they knew the format this would take and the requirements that would be made of them and their service.

It seemed the hospital and some local men who were off fighting in the war were never far from each other's thoughts. The children in Forelands had done their duty on Empire Day by sending servicemen some much needed cigarettes. One soldier, Private W.H., himself a previous patient at the hospital, replied, thanking them.

During the war, the hospital had seen an unprecedented growth and demands on its services. It is amazing that, amongst the bombs and rationing that war imposed, the staff and committee managed to keep the hospital going as well as they did. In fact, from 1934 to 1944, in-patients rose from 5,175 to 9,247 and out-patients 72,736 to 126,153.

Partial advert for subscriptions, 1940. Courtesy of The Royal Orthopaedic hospital, Birmingham, NHS Trust.

Following D-Day and the end of the war, many servicemen returned to the area, necessitating treatment, leading to surgeons being diverted away from their 'Cripple Hospital' duties to this new concern, resulting in some clinic closures. In 1945, the Cadbury family were once again offering help by giving up part of their homes to accommodate some nurses. There were nurses, at the time, sleeping in the condemned administration block as well as using buildings in Bristol Road.

Due to the Blitz, the many hospitals in the city were inundated with casualties as well as having to cope with the normal influx of patients requiring medical help and surgery. They had to prepare and make space for those servicemen requiring medical and surgical assistance too. Staff, resources and the buildings themselves were stretched to the limit, often being the victims of the *Luftwaffe's* attentions.

CHAPTER THIRTEEN

Read All About It

The local newspapers, despite the problem of censorship and reduction in the availability of paper, did a good job of keeping the people of Birmingham up to date with not only the latest war developments but also what was happening locally to help the war effort.

They did their very best to boost the morale of the local populace. One of the ways the *Birmingham Mail* did this was to produce a column that tackled a different aspect every week. One column focused on the issue of resolve, pointing out that it was the resolve of the British people that had seen them honour their pledge to Poland and take a stand against Germany.

The thrust of this column was setting the tone for the New Year (1940) in that it urged readers to find their resolve and 'bend all our energy in the coming twelve months to the defeat of the "evil things" implicit in the name of Nazism'.

Thoughts also turned to what would happen after the war and that resolve was needed to find a way forward and rebuild what had been lost, more so than at the end of the Great War.

Living in Birmingham during the war was certainly no picnic but even the paper had its humorous side, to lighten the mood and help people through it. It would often publish jokes, poking fun at the dire times. One such joke, embedded in an advert, involved barrage balloons:

> *Why do the barrage balloons go up and down? So that their crews can leave them occasionally to go and buy some Taverner Rutledge Old English Fruit Drops.*

There were several smaller articles and items in each issue of the *Birmingham Mail* that sought to inform and tickle the funny bones of its readers. One such item was talking about the 'busy day' the twenty German officers were going to have who had gone to Russia to help sort out the Russian Army, inferring not only were the German officers not up to the job but the Russian Army was beyond help.

They commented on the various orders and regulations that came into force throughout the duration of the war. Their overriding sentiment was 'we shall survive'. Patriotism and just getting on with it were the actions they wanted their readers to adopt. There had been a lot of talk about rationing and the measures that could be taken, and now they were rapidly coming into force. It was suggested that the people of Birmingham should be proud to do their bit and that a little bit of cutting down was for the good of the country and the war. 'Why grumble?' was the question often posed. There was a lot worse going on abroad and the people of Birmingham were expected to be thankful for their lot. The paper billed rationing as also having health benefits for the whole nation and that, finally, being wasteful was targeted. They harked back to the food queues of the First World War and said to avoid that scenario they should be prepared to cut back.

The paper was full of useful information like the current blackout times that were prepared by the Astronomer Royal. On Saturday 6 June 1940, the blackout ran from 4.41pm to 7.46am.

The paper also had an opinion on the financial plans of Birmingham City Council, which claimed they required a five-year period to pay for the ARP. The paper thought they were being a little too optimistic and that it would take a far longer period.

One interesting snippet on 11 January 1940 was to do with the population of Germany. It was said that the Germans were 'boasting' about the number of babies that were being born in their country compared with Great Britain and France together. They claimed to have had 300,000 births in 1939. The paper's reply to that was, 'Well, they all have to be fed, don't they?' alluding to the rationing and shortages in place.

At the end of the war, the focus turned to demobilisation and a controversial plan was drawn-up by Ernest Bevin. The papers, as we see in Chapter 14, were inundated with letters from concerned readers who felt the plan was not going to get their husbands, sweethearts, sons or fathers back quick enough. They also published their own response to the plan.

In a section that looked back over the six-year period of the war, its readers' immediate response was one of relief and gratitude that the war was finally over. But when thoughts turned to the state of the nation and the uphill struggle it was going to be to rebuild and recover, it was of little comfort when rationing was to continue and most of the men couldn't yet get home.

They spoke of the 'pride' in British 'doggedness, pluck and perseverance', that had once again given them victory. The fact that there had been far less casualties and deaths this time compared to the First World War was pleasing to the *Birmingham Mail* and must have been of great comfort to those whose loved ones were safe, awaiting passage home.

There was still caution in the fact that weaponry had been taken to a new level with the appearance of the atomic bomb and rockets, but it was hoped that through the devastation seen from this war, there should be no more wars. Instead, they felt this was a great opportunity for the world to better the lives of everyone. There should be forward movement not backwards.

The descendants of those veterans who fought in the Great War were on the minds of the *Birmingham Mail* as they hoped they wouldn't have to go through anything like what their grandparents and parents had done, or worse, in years to come. It was seen as the duty of everyone to ensure this didn't happen.

CHAPTER FOURTEEN

Dear Sir and Letters Home

The local newspapers of the time carried many letters to the editor, which give a fantastic insight into the mood of the people of Birmingham. The letters highlighted what was on the minds of the population and what bothered them as well as what delighted them.

One subject often written about in such letters was that of evacuation and the closure and re-opening of schools in the city. One disgruntled reader was questioning the wisdom of re-opening Saltley Secondary School for just a couple of hours on a Friday. The reader felt this did not fit in with the message of reducing waste from the government. He was concerned about the heating costs and waste of fuel.

Allotments, or a lack of them, was a hot topic. One reader was incensed that he'd seen numerous posters and leaflets around the city extolling people to dig for victory, yet Solihull Council had yet to process his application or allocate him some land, which he'd sent in last September (it was now January 1940). He accused the council of 'hibernating' and urged for them to be 'stirred into action'.

People, mainly members serving in the armed forces abroad, would often send letters of thanks for the goods and letters they received from the people of Birmingham. One BEF commanding officer had this to say:

> It has been a great source of pleasure to know that the city to which we are proud to belong and which is home to us all, should have remembered us in so practical a manner this Christmas.

He said that he wouldn't forget the motto of Birmingham: Forward.

Another military man, Lord Willoughby de Broke, wrote to the *Birmingham Mail* for 605 County of Warwick Squadron in the RAF. He hoped they would soon be back in Castle Bromwich under 'happier conditions'.

One man, based at a 'Midland RAF station', was thankful for the comforts they had received and wanted to make local people aware that they would 'do all in their power to be worthy of all the confidence reposed in them'.

Being in the armed forces and preparing to go to war at any moment was as difficult for the men as it was for those left behind. The fact that the people of Birmingham were thinking about those of their inhabitants who were away, fighting and

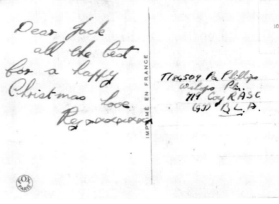

Christmas postcard sent by Reginald Phillips to his friend Jock in the early 1940s. Courtesy of David Phillips.

*Original envelope from 1944, when Reginald Phillips was in Liverpool.
Courtesy of David Phillips.*

protecting the city and the country, made the situation a whole lot
easier for them.

Often, organisations and establishments would use the
letters page of the local press to give information to readers.
The Birmingham Corporation did this on numerous occasions
throughout the war. One such letter informed readers about the
salvage of waste paper and card. They were reminding readers,
prompted by a previous letter from 'Anxious to Help', that there
was a Ministry of Supply Scheme in force with the names and
addresses of where local collection points were. People could also
contact the local boy scouts, who would come and remove the waste
paper and card. The main address was given as The Birmingham
Waste Co Ltd at Moland Mills, Belmont Row.

There was another letter on this subject advising that the
residents of Birmingham had asked people to bind their waste
paper into bundles and place them on top of bins on collection

days, or to give them to the dustman. Now they were calling on the help of housewives to also place out old carpets, sacking, etc, for the dustmen too, as well as non-ferrous metals.

They were reminded that the facilities for the recycling and disposal of refuse were some of the most sophisticated in the country, that they sell £2,397-worth of materials (£40,000) reclaimed from the refuse, and that they were committed to making 'wealth from waste'.

This was a call to arms for housewives from the general manager of the Birmingham Salvage Department, J.H. Codling.

We have seen many examples of how motorists came a cropper with the lighting orders and this didn't escape the notice of the read-

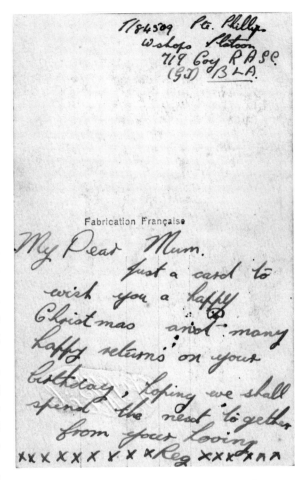

Joint Christmas card and birthday card sent by Reginald Phillips to his mother Val while he was away in the forces. Courtesy of Reginald Phillips.

ers of the *Birmingham Mail*. One person, not a local man, who had been driving from Scotland to Preston and then Birmingham, was incensed by the state of the roads the nearer he got to the city. Due to the fog, visibility was low and, because of that and the dirty white lines on the road, he had difficulty driving. He compared the roads in Scotland with those into the city and said those in Scotland were marked appropriately, and clean, to greatly assist

Se chiudo gli occhi il viso tuo m'appar
come quella sera nel cerchio del fanal...
Tutte le notti sogno allor
di ritornar... di riposar...
con te, Lili Marlen
con te, Lili Marlen.

French postcard, early 1940s. Author's own.

drivers since the blackout began. He advised the council to sort it out before more accidents occurred.

Conscription was a controversial subject. W. Attwood-Evans from Quinton did not like the fact that some people, both in parliament and in the streets, were against conscription, who called it a 'thorny problem'. According to the writer conscription presented two issues, the first of which was a national one. He reminded readers that Great Britain had been caught on the hop at the beginning of the Great War and were woefully prepared. He feared that should war break out for a third time, 'democracy will be swallowed in the victory of an aggressor.'

The achievement of world peace was considered impossible without the use of force against the aggressor. He saw conscription as necessary to achieve a strong and capable armed forces.

But conscription didn't just have an effect nationally, it was also personal. The writer said he felt most people who were against

Embroidered card from France, 1940. Author's own.

A PRAYER FOR YOU IS SAID TODAY
FOR ALL THE PERILS OF YOUR WAY
AT HOME, ABROAD, – LAND, SEA & AIR
MAY GOD'S GUIDING HAND PROTECT
YOU THERE.

Card sent to Reginald Phillips from his family, while he was in the forces. Courtesy of David Phillips.

conscription were so because it hampered freedom of the person being conscripted, and it stopped them going about their usual daily business. He thought that the routines and discipline of the armed forces didn't harm most youths.

In reply, another writer, who was an ex-Territorial and army man, was not pleased with what he had said, especially his comments about army life and youths, stating that the letter was 'utter nonsense and shows his ignorance of service life'. He went on to say that Britain couldn't possibly ensure the peace of the world whether they had conscription or not.

Training, such as that received in the services, was only good for dogs, was his opinion, and he encouraged the writer to go along to his nearest recruitment office and join-up, telling him to practice what he preached, regardless of his age. If it was good enough for the youths it was good enough for the writer.

The letters still flooded in, albeit on different subjects, even when the war ended. The focus on the minds of Birmingham inhabitants was primarily the painfully slow demobilisation process. At the end of the war there were many thousands of men who had served in the armed forces still abroad, and bringing them home was going to be a logistical and financial problem.

The Minister of Labour and National Service Ernest Bevin came up with a plan that would allow personnel to be demobilised at different stages, which would be calculated on their age and length of service. Special consideration was given to married men and women over the age of fifty as well as those who had skills and experience in the various jobs back home that were needed to be filled in to start rebuilding Britain.

For many in Birmingham, the announcement of Bevin's plan was the final straw and they wrote in to the *Birmingham Mail* to vent their frustration.

One ex-serviceman of the ATS, Kingstanding, had been reading previous letters about demobilisation and taken offence at their disrespect for war-workers. He pointed out that, although there were some men who went into the munitions factories at the outbreak of war, most of the workforce in such places was already there and so therefore could not enlist. There were concerns as to whether those in the armed forces who had been promised jobs when they returned would actually have jobs to go to given the amount of people employed to replace them whilst they were fighting. The writer of the letter wanted the men to come home as quickly as possible, but that the war-workers were not the reason for the delay.

A woman, whose husband had been away fighting, stated that 'love is a woman's whole existence' and that women who had families and could care for their homes could 'face any crisis and make any sacrifice'. She pointed out that women had shouldered a lot of the responsibility and hardship of war, particularly the 'incessant worry and anxiety and the awful, gnawing loneliness'. She didn't feel that the delay in getting all the men home and prolonging the women's suffering was fair. She said: 'Hitler himself could not have designed a more cruel, iniquitous, soul-crushing form of torture than the present demob plan.' The letter was signed Quite Desperate – Moseley.

Another reader was keen to state that the demobilisation plan had a flaw in that it was keeping much-needed skilled workers from returning to the workforce. Her husband was a builder's manager before he enlisted, but in the army he was a driver-operator with the Royal Artillery in Italy. He had written to her lamenting his current role of various odd jobs. He said:

> I might be helping to build houses in England and I'm watering flowers in Italy.

One letter from a reader, who called himself Still Fighting (RASC), was concerned about the wives of servicemen having to carry on without their husbands and was frustrated that, while the men were stuck abroad, the war-workers, who he saw as 'enjoying' high wages and the comforts of home, were sitting in the servicemen's jobs. He said:

> The serviceman has been sacrificed on the Altar of war for six years. What is to be his reward? A further sacrifice upon the altar of peace?

He wanted a level playing field with a fair chance of getting a job on his return so he could 'improve the home life of our families'. He saw the only way to do that was to speed up the demobilisation process.

Still on the subject of demobilisation, another writer, A True Conservative, from Tipton, admonished the Labour Party for what he saw as their part in reneging on their pre-election promises. The fact that demobilisation was not going to happen quickly was a great disappointment to a lot of people.

As many other writers also pointed out, there were implications because of the munition workers who had to be found new jobs, and this was what was seen as hampering the servicemen's homecoming. He raised the question as to why the munitions workers were seemingly taking precedence over the men in the forces. In his opinion, talking about the munition workers, 'A little unemployment and low pay' couldn't do them much harm and he was aghast at how the brave men who fought for their country would be taking second place to men who had 'stayed at home in comfort'.

Many people, including one reader of the *Birmingham Mail*, thought that the servicemen waiting to come home had been let down by the government and reminded the government that it was servicemen votes that had seen Labour elected and they should do the right thing by them.

Another serviceman's wife wrote to the paper, giving readers his views, on his behalf, on the delays faced in demobilisation:

> *The wind has been taken out of our sails and the atmosphere became exceedingly tense. It is impossible to describe the disappointment and bitterness out here, and we are hoping and expecting that reaction at home will not allow things to remain as they are.*

There was controversy over the Ministry of Works' thinking about inviting women to work in the building trade. This, according to one writer was not on and they suggested that the many men who were 'eating their hearts out' in the forces abroad, and who had much more experience and were skilled, would be a better solution to the lack of manpower in the building trade. He urged the government to not employ women but to let these men come back home instead. It would be no reward to the men if the women took their jobs.

Of course, families, businesses and trades wanted their men back as soon as possible, but the problem Birmingham Council had at the time was lots of ex-servicemen coming home but nowhere to accommodate them, and the feeling was that the women had stepped up to the plate and earned their right to work.

Demobilisation was causing concerns when it came to housing and, according to one writer, some of the estate agents in Birmingham were obviously unimpressed with servicemen seeking homes, and that the offending agents had nevertheless been appreciative of the RAF's protection during the Battle of Britain when the property they were selling was in danger.

The writer had been looking for a house while he was on leave, but an ill-mannered estate agent hadn't even had the good grace to speak to him direct and had sent out a girl to pass on the message that there was 'nothing to discuss'. He then tried somewhere else, only to be met with a similar 'rude' attitude from another estate agent, who would only let people view properties if they came into the office on a weekly basis. 'Presumably, levitation is considered part of the RAF training!' he said.

All he asked was for the servicemen who had done the job they were supposed to do be shown consideration and that something should be done to speed up the requisitioning of empty properties that were being sold at a hiked price, just because they were empty.

Other war-related topics that had the readers of the *Birmingham Mail* writing in was that of the Dig for Victory campaign and the restrained face by land-lease supplies. One reader was concerned about how the war impacted on foreign trade. D.C. Hague thought 'we must export or perish'. The fact that Great Britain had less than modern machinery and plant when the USA had much more mechanisation was a bone of contention. He claimed that any savings made for the war had been expended and that we now needed a further fundraising drive to pay for more, newer and faster machinery to get the wheels of British trade and industry moving again.

Education and the disruption the war had meant for their children was also a popular theme to letters. One school, in Solihull, amongst other measures, as a form of educational reform, was going to stop fee-paying. Many people were aghast at this suggestion, which one reader, Younger Generation from Smethwick, called 'snobbery'. He pointed out that they had just come through a war that should have made people think that the traditional school system had to change. He felt that abolishing school fees was a way forward to greater equality and opportunity in education.

Another issue written about in the letters pages was that of the clothing ration. There had been rumours going around that it was only because Great Britain had a socialist government. The writer, from Acocks Green, begged to differ. They pointed out that there were a lot of men due home from fighting who would have ninety clothing coupons each as well as the civilian ration cards. They were therefore 'proud' to have to go without for a longer time so that the men coming home had enough.

Birmingham had just been through horrendous bombardments. Night after night loud and destructive bombs had fallen, causing much damage and many roaring fires with sirens wailing to alert its inhabitants to the incoming danger. Now this danger was over, one contributor to the letters page complained about the 'loud speaker nuisance'. They were referring to the recent election campaigning vehicles with their loud speakers blaring through the streets of Birmingham as well as vans advertising the bus strikes. They felt that the open-air VJ celebrations taking part in the city, with loud music and dancing into the early hours, along with loud music and announcements from sports fields, was too much.

The writer, from Shirley in Solihull, thought that people were complaining of tiredness because they couldn't sleep or rest in their homes due to the noise and was hopeful that the appropriate authorities would take action 'before we are all reduced to nervous wrecks'. Given the ear-shattering explosions of the bombs, one would think that many of the inhabitants of the city were already nervous wrecks.

Another regular section in the *Birmingham Mail* was the Day by Day column that kept Birmingham informed of the everyday goings on in the war. In 1945 there had been much talk about pensions in London, something the authorities in the city were keen to get information about. Both Captain Blackburn, MP for Kings Norton, and Fred Longden, MP for Deritend, had questioned James Griffiths, the Minister of National Insurance, on the subject.

Neither man was happy with the way the government seemed to be proceeding on the issue of pensions, and Mr Longden had written to the minister. Mr Griffiths, in his reply, cited staff and accommodation shortages as hampering the government's plans.

CHAPTER FIFTEEN

Local Lads and Ladies

So many men from Birmingham fought in the Second World War and so many women were integral to the war effort that it would be impossible to document all their names and stories here. But this chapter will look at a couple of men who fought, some of the women, and the efforts they and their families made to keep in contact with each other – a comfort in the dark days of the Blitz and the fierce fighting abroad. These letters provide an interesting insight into what was going on during the war and how the authors of the letters felt about things.

In the Second World War, letters were the only form of communication families had. One family were the Greaves and their son, Ken, Second-Lieutenant K.C. Greaves, served with the 231 Light AA Battery RA in the Middle East.

One of his first letters to his parents was rather a long one, as he had been saving up his news to fill a whole letter. It is dated 5 October 1941. He describes his sailing over there and adds: 'I can now tell you a few things it would have been unwise to include in the letters I wrote to you while we were waiting to sail.'

He was waiting at the harbour at Clyde with the rest of the convey before they sailed and reported an air of great excitement. He said he wouldn't have missed the day they sailed for the world, as all the crews of all the ships were out on their decks:

> *It was quite the most impressive, awe inspiring sight I ever hope to see – and one of the most beautiful too. There was a grand full moon. All around us was magnificent country, looking all the better for the moonlight, and also for the fact that we wouldn't see it again for some time.*

Ken then went on to describe the first few hours of the journey:

> *We could see most of the ships quite plainly, then one by one navigation lights appeared on their mast heads and on their bridges. Then in a few minutes the destroyers and other naval vessels came by and went out of the harbour to make sure everything was alright for us to move off. A few more minutes and the rattle from our anchor chain was heard as the first ship prepared to leave and then great excitement as we could see her moving out towards the harbour entrance. Then another ship and with a huge rattle, up came our anchor, bells rang here and there and slowly we moved away. With binoculars, we watched the other ships move out behind us, and watched their navigation lights go out as they reached the harbour mouth. We stopped on deck a long time, and one by one went reluctantly to bed – it was such a magnificent sight that we could have stopped there indefinitely.*

Crossing of the Line Ceremony aboard the Empress of Russia, *1940. The crossing of the line ceremony is a Naval rite of initiation to celebrate when a sailor first crosses the equator. Courtesy of Caroline Bagnall.*

The general feeling at the time appeared to be of excitement and adventure, and not the fear of what might come. In fact, the voyage took place without incident. Ken's only complaint after consuming a five-course breakfast on board, consisting of, amongst other things, grapefruit and then some marmalade, was that those preparing and serving the breakfast didn't know how to make tea.

He described the amazing sights around him:

> *Up on deck, again, there was our convoy – the grandest sight imaginable. Big ships, medium ships and little ships, all in neat straight lines, ploughing merrily along together, dipping their boughs deep into the waves and then coming up again with white surf streaming down them. And all around the convoy are the destroyers steaming along with a great white bow wave, every now and then shooting off here and there among the convoy at lighting speed. They certainly inspire confidence as they come past with their guns ready and their decks heaped with depth charges.*

Despite the risks around them they still managed to let off a little steam! Courtesy of Caroline Bagnall.

But their voyage wasn't completely without risk, as Ken explained:

Sometimes one of our planes would come out to have a look at us. One day Jerry did the same, but the Navy soon dealt with him, and he got nowhere very near the convey at all.

The voyages were long but far from feeling bored and itching to see some action, the entertainment on board kept them occupied:

Last Sunday we had a very successful service again – and we managed a psalm this time – and at night we had a grand hour of community hymn singing. I hope to do another next week, and also an evening of ordinary community singings – songs by Traditional and Anonymous instead of Henry Hall, etc.

Henry Hall was famous as a British band-leader from the 1920s to the 1950s and penned the song *The Teddy Bear's Picnic* in 1932. He also played to the troops in the Second World War:

Last night I put on a Battery concert which was quite successful; including a very amateur violin rendering of Ave Maria *and a recitation by a typical cockney of* the Green Eye of the Little Yellow God. *I have also been doing a bit of unarmed combat, and the O.C. already has a nasty bruise on his elbow – much to the delight of the blokes.*

One of Ken's other jobs onboard was to censor letters, which he found quite amusing:

One man wrote today that he had been seasick and that it was terrible to have been "vomitating" all day.

He again signed off his letter by asking them not to worry, to which he added: 'I am having the time of my life!'

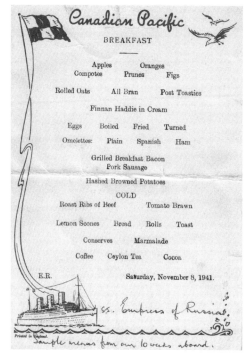
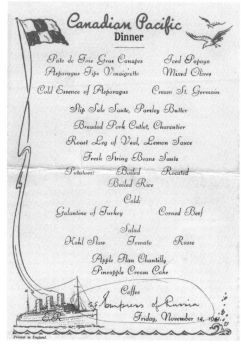

Canadian Pacific dinner menu, 1941. Courtesy of Caroline Bagnall.

Interestingly he also signs this letter off with 'Love to all, particularly Mrs Ward'. According to the letter-keeper this was a pre-arranged code that meant the ship was getting near to West Africa.

In one letter, dated 4 December 1941, he says this:

Dear Mother and Dad

At last we have reached our destination, and it is a change to look round and see, instead of nothing but sea, nothing but sand. We had a very pleasant and interesting voyage and I hope you have received some of my letters from our few points of call. We are in quite a comfortable camp and are settling down to soldiering once more… We have not received any mail but look forward to getting some fairly soon.

Realising that his parents would be worried about him, he was keen to reassure them:

There is no need to worry about me. I am perfectly fit and well out of harm's way.

Ken was also obviously thinking about his family back home:

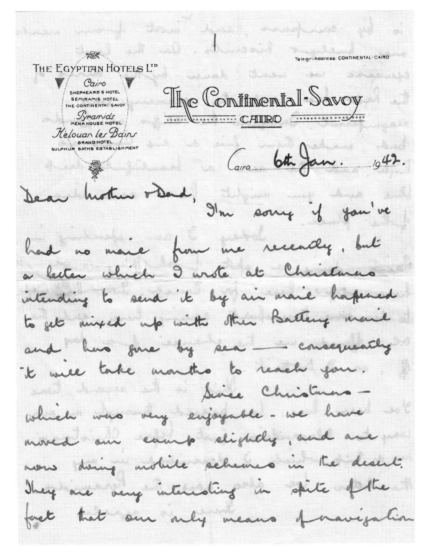

Letter from Ken to his mother and father on the Continental-Savoy Hotel, Cairo, note paper, 1942. Courtesy of Caroline Bagnall.

I hope all at home are still okay. Is Sid still going strong?
I hope we will be home for Christmas.

He advised his parents to write by airmail, as it was quicker than the land post.

His mother wrote back to him from the family home in Tamworth Road, Sutton Coldfield, and told him about the bombing raids in Birmingham:

Letter from Ken's mother, mentioning the bombings in Birmingham, 1940. Courtesy of Caroline Bagnall.

Last night we had another warning and could hear guns but not too near to us and in the distance, could see a great glow from a big fire somewhere. Today I have heard from one or two that the centre of town is in a terrible state. Fires at Marshalls and C & As – Boots Chemist's in New Street and the Dolcis Boot Shop. The Imperial Music

Hall and several places in that district. They said a fire at first was started at the Paramount but they dealt with that and quickly prevented it spreading. But when they fired Marshalls it must have gone rapidly and lady who told me about it said from what her husband said it would have to be rebuilt.

I expect they will bring some news tonight when family return. All New Street is full of hose pipes and no traffic anywhere in centre of town. Mary said the PO had refused any parcels unless for anyone on active service today. There was a mention of damage to Birmingham PO, isn't it terrible? There is only one thing there would be no lives lost in places like that after business hours. Our first siren was about 8.

Even though the sirens and bomb damage was apparent, the family were keen to point out that life was also still going on despite all this:

Mary and Philip are going to wedding of Hilda Brookes and Mr Marshall at Castle Bromwich at 2.30 tomorrow. Last night after David had gone to bed, Mary had to go up to him – he said Papa wants me I'm giggling. When the siren goes if he isn't asleep we have him down and dad has nursed him for a bit. The night before he said the sirens make me feel bad.

For a Birmingham lad, used to the hustle and bustle and sprawling industrial city landscape, to be suddenly in the sands of Cairo, of which he would probably only ever have seen photographs in school textbooks, it must have come as a bit of a shock:

It is a very quaint place. Camels wander along the streets; and the harbour is alive with picturesque rowing boats and magnificent dhows (a traditional sailing boat), which look as old as the hills. There are plenty of hills too – great bare chunks of rock, worn by the weather into curious shapes. And past the hills one can see just miles and miles of red sand, and in the distance, are more hills. The hills round the harbour are really magnificent – if you saw them on screen you would immediately say they were made of plaster and couldn't possibly be real.

He also had a friend, a nurse called Betty, who before the war had worked with eight nurses. She hadn't seen them since, only to find four of them where they had landed. The reunion prompted a party and Ken discovered that one of the nurses had married the chief of police there, and he found him interesting to talk to.

He finished this letter by saying:

By the time you get this I suppose Hitler will have been thoroughly thrashed in the Western Desert, and I sincerely hope that we will be in time to put our oar in before it is all over. Once he is beaten there, providing all goes well in Russia, he won't last too long. I hope you are all fit and well at home and not getting too much attention from Jerry. I am as fit as ever, and of course we are all anxious to give Jerry a Christmas present.

In the interests of national security and to ensure the positions of the navy and army were kept hidden from the enemy as far as possible, letters were censored, as was the one Ken wrote. Consequently, families back home were often unsure as to where their menfolk were fighting abroad. In one letter, Ken alluded to this fact by saying:

I am allowed to tell you that we have been 'somewhere in South Africa'.

It was quite the cleanest city I have ever visited, and I think one of the most beautiful too. Apart from the fact that the palm trees grow along most roads, that negroes in the most fantastic costumes rushed along the roads pulling rickshaws, and that there was no blackout, it might easily have been an English town … We sailed into town in the morning (with the memorable signal at our masthead, 'Look out X………, here we come). And when the blokes went ashore in the afternoon there were crowds of civilians at the dock gates ready to take them sight-seeing and probably home to dinner as well.

This letter showed that it wasn't always a case of hard work and fighting when abroad. Ken wasn't on duty for the duration of his stay there and described how he filled his time:

I spent a very pleasant few days knocking about the place in a quiet, lazy sort of way. Most nights we had dinner at a very pleasant hotel in the town, and either sat gossiping on the veranda overlooking the sea or went out to a sort of road house place and danced in the open air. It was a grand place full of palm trees (which in turn were full of monkeys) and it overlooked a magnificent beach.

Needless to say, I was not alone on these excursions, and while all the blokes were going round being polite to the O.C. I was having a much better time with my nurse friend!!

He also was aware, however, of the restrictions he faced whilst serving:

I did quite a lot of shopping while ashore, and among other things bought myself a camera, and I hope to make myself a record of my travels, although of course I shall be restricted to a certain extent by regulations.

A letter dated 6 December 1941 wishes his mother a happy birthday, but due to the delay in the post he was aware that the letter wouldn't reach her until afterwards. Having enjoyed shopping and wandering round where he was stationed, he was now getting more accustomed to the weather:

I am writing this in the middle of a dust storm which has already lasted over two hours. Everything is covered in fine sand which penetrates everything. My bed is full of it as is my trunk. My hair is full of it and my throat is practically dry.

The dry, hot weather obviously wasn't the only thing that worried him. The local wildlife had been making an unwelcome appearance too:

> Last night I played my recorder but no snakes turned up. They don't seem to appreciate Brahms' Cradle Song. Perhaps they prefer the drums which the native troops nearby beat incessantly all night long.

Thoughts of home were never far from his mind, either: 'Next year we'll celebrate with a game of snooker (oh for a game!!!).'

Music was also important in Ken's life, and something he loved to encourage participation in with the rest of the troops as well as appreciating the musical gifts sent by his family:

> I was thrilled to get a letter from you yesterday, together with the magazines and copies of Cyril's song ... I have been singing "There's No Place Like England" so much during the last twenty-four hours that Robert Hodd who shares my tent is starting to sing it too. This afternoon I played it on my recorder ... If it had only arrived a fortnight earlier I could have put it in the pantomime ... Don't let Marjorie forget that she promised me that she would arrange a two - pianos recital for R.B. too. I hope the Crackerjax came up to their usual standard – if they can provide their own transport I will fix a date out here for them.

The level of entertainment for the troops, in the opinion of Ken, was very good and varied:

> We are going to the cinema tonight at a local aerodrome. Some of the cinemas here are very quaint – a screen, some seats, and four walls; no roof. Others are very good, built to very modern designs in clay, or very occasionally with bricks and mortar. I've not yet been to a show, although I used to be able to lie in bed and listen to the film at the cinema about three-quarters of a mile away.

He was keen to describe the walks he went on and the scenery he took in – painting a picture of the environment for his family back home in Birmingham:

*Not far from us is a big range of mountains in the form
of an escarpment with sheer cliffs down one side. There is
hardly any way through them, and on a scheme recently
we set out to "blaze a trail" round behind them. It was
very hard going and by lunchtime we were about half way
with the most difficult bit still before us. I also had the
job of going back to camp to collect another gun and then
re-joining the troop. Consequently, I set off after lunch
(Bully Beef and biscuits, and very good too) with a tractor
and gun detachment to push on as hard as I could. All our
navigation in the desert of course is done by compass, and
we decided on our route over lunch.*

Ken mentions in the letter that they had discovered two ways to
get through. One route, the shortest, was deemed too risky but he
had seen a wadi – or valley – that he thought was worth the risk.
He was concerned they might get stuck in the sand with no one to
find them and help get them out. When they came to the top of the
hill, there was a problem – a 100–150ft drop. They carefully edged
around and were able to get down the steep side. But he had been
right to be concerned about the sand.

*Again and again we nearly got stuck and all the blokes
had to get out and shove. Once we got so badly "bogged"
in the sand that with all the chaps pushing and the engine
revving as hard as she could go we were only just moving
forward at all, and we kept that up for about twenty yards;
until just as I thought I couldn't possibly push for another
second the tyres began to bite on harder ground, we moved
more quickly as we got out.*

They eventually made it back to camp and all was well, if hard
going. He went on to start reminiscing about the roads back home.

*Driving through the desert is no picnic. Oh to be back
in England for a good blind along tarmac roads, where
far from needing a compass, a scale and a protractor,
and iron rations "just in case" – one doesn't even need
a map!*

It's interesting to see from Ken's letter to his parents how he and they approached Christmas. Rationing was in full swing at home, and with Ken being desert-based, his Christmas was going to be a world away from the traditional celebrations he was used to at home:

I'm glad you had a good Christmas and managed to get a turkey and most of the usual bits and pieces. We had a grand time out here. The men had turkey, stuffing, roast potatoes, etc., plum pudding, mince pies free beer and free cigarettes. The mess tent was decorated with coloured streamers, and the meal was preceded by a mock Battery parade.

While Ken enjoyed the more exotic fruits abroad, his family could have only dreamed of such delights:

My own dinner on Boxing Day was a great success and there was certainly no shortage of fruit and nuts (I suppose I must eat on average about four oranges per day!) I had to recite my latest poem about the Regiment entitled "Alf (i.e. Flash Alf the Colonel) and his light Ack Ack Gunners", which was quite successful. It is a parody on the lion and Albert.

New Year's Day I spent in a lorry on an aerodrome in the desert. We were on a scheme and were deployed around the place for the night. It was so cold that neither me or Robert could sleep, and we spent the night walking up and down to keep warm. The first time we got up and clambered out of the truck feeling like nothing on earth we were greeted by a sentry who said, "Happy New Year, Sir," And we gathered that the New Year was in.

It was a poor way of celebrating "Hogmany" [sic] but the chaps took it very well. A hundred yards away was an RAF canteen in which there was a terrific party going on. But not one of our blokes complained or asked permission to leave his position to go over there, and the only remark we heard all night was when a half-plastered RAF bloke came out of the canteen and one of our blokes yelled in beautifully cheerful cockney, "What's the beer like, mate?"

Ken had no qualms about the quality of the men in the troop:

> *They really are a first-rate crowd. They know how to work and what's more they know how to laugh: and when the time comes they'll jolly well show Jerry how to shoot.*

He also told his parents about the stranger aspects of desert life:

> *I've seen plenty of mirages, in fact every time you go into the desert you see them. You see huge lakes a few miles away, and even if you use field glasses they look quite real. They are the result, of course, of the sort of heat haze caused by the sun on the sand.*

He again mentions the local wildlife, which was nothing like the sort of wildlife he was used to at home, although living in the city, the wild open spaces of the desert and the many different creatures that inhabited it would have been a revelation to Ken:

> *A few nights ago, I was awakened by a pack of jackals howling in the district. I saw one about a week ago, and set off the next day with a rifle to look for him, but was unlucky. There are also a few small gazelles in the desert; and little lizards dart about in the sand.*

Ken was released from military duty with the rank of captain on 22 August 1946.

Women did a great deal for the war effort, whether they worked in munitions factories, Cadbury and Bournville's as part of the ATS or women's services, nurses or ARP, they rose to the challenge. The work of the ARP was often challenging and extremely dangerous, undertaken in dire situations with poor equipment. There are many reports in the local press and wider sources about the heroic efforts of ARP personnel throughout the war, far too many to document here, but one event that occurred during a particularly heavy bombardment on the night of 19 November 1940 is notable.

This incident, during a bombing raid. shows the courage and determination of just one local lady. In St Paul's Road, an ARP warden, Mrs Beatrice Withers, who was in her fifties, was on duty. She became concerned for the health of one of the women

P/155406   22nd August, 1946

Sir,

Now that the time has come for your release from active military duty, I am commanded by the Army Council to express to you their thanks for the valuable services which you have rendered in the service of your country at a time of grave national emergency.

At the end of the emergency you will relinquish your commission, and at that time a notification will appear in the London Gazette (Supplement), granting you also the honorary rank of Captain. Meanwhile, you have permission to use that rank with effect from the date of your release.

I am, Sir,

Your obedient Servant,

Captain K.C. Greaves,
    Royal Artillery.

Ken's release from active military duty certificate. Courtesy of Caroline Bagnall.

living on the road who had given birth recently, thinking she may have developed an infection. Beatrice walked to the nearest ARP station to telephone for assistance. As she was waiting for the ambulance, back in St Paul's Road, the bombardment commenced with screamers – a type of high explosive bomb with a whistle attached to the fin, so it made a dreadful noise to frighten people as it descended.

At 9pm that evening, one of the inhabitants of the road (21 St Paul's Road), Dennis Sharpe, who was aged 14, was seen by Beatrice as he watched the bombs and the anti-aircraft guns and the glow from the city. She instructed him to go back into the house as he would be safer in the cellar where his step-mum Edith Sharpe and dad Alfred were, as well as other members of this large family.

Edith had been married before but lost her previous husband, Frederick Carey, in 1926. She married Alfred, who had also had a previous marriage in 1913. The family now lived together in St Paul's Road. During other raids, the family usually took refuge in one of the public shelters nearby. But on this night, due to Edith suffering from a cold and the advice from the authorities not to go into public shelters if they were ill, to help prevent the spread of disease, the family stayed at home, in the cellar. Thankfully, not all of them were at home that night.

May, their 11-year-old daughter, was away at the Princess Alice Orphanage, New Oscott, because there hadn't been any room in St Paul's Road for her. There were other family members away in the forces too. But, Jesse, aged 18, another daughter, who had been with May at the orphanage, was now back home, as was a son John Sharpe aged 21, with three Carey children – Frederick (24), Joyce (21) and Raymond (17).

Many of the other houses in the road were vacant as their inhabitants had gone to stay with friends and relatives elsewhere out of the city. But at number 24, two sisters, the Abels, were sitting on the cellar steps sharing cups of tea as their Anderson shelter was flooded and unusable.

At around 9pm, everything changed for these families forever. A huge explosion occurred, scattering lethal shards of shrapnel everywhere. A bomb had hit the Sharpes' back garden. One of these large fragments cut into Beatrice's helmet and head, rendering her unconscious. The two Abel sisters were blown down the steps of the cellar. The blast had only wounded Beatrice and as she woke, bleeding heavily, she blew her whistle to call for help. The bomb had taken out ten houses, including the Sharpes'.

Knowing her duty and responsibilities, Beatrice with Mr Poole, a senior warden, fought their way through the debris of the destroyed house of the woman she had called the ambulance for. They found the sick woman and her baby and were able to drag them out, taking them and four other children to a shelter.

Although Beatrice was wounded, she declined medical aid for herself and went back to the scene of the blast. A local police officer, PC Derek Taylor, was on the scene and had managed to rescue the two Abel sisters while Beatrice and other rescue workers attempted to search the other houses. Because the bomb had hit the Sharpes' back garden, the house had suffered severe damage and it took hours to get through the rubble. Luckily, they were able to rescue some of the family but, sadly, not all of them.

Edith Sharpe had fallen across her 4-year-old daughter Marjorie, who had survived and was uninjured. All three Careys had perished in the blast, as had Dennis and John Sharpe. Edith's husband Alfred and daughter Jesse had survived but were badly injured. Alfred was taken to Hollymoor Emergency Hospital, but died on 1 December. Jesse also passed away on 20 November. There were reported to be nine deaths and many more injured from that incident alone.

Tragedies like this played out up and down the city, night after night. If it hadn't been for the bravery and determination of the ARP and other volunteers and professionals such as the police, the survival rate amongst those caught in the Blitz would have been much lower. Beatrice was rewarded for her actions with the BEM – British Empire Medal.

Another lad who fought in the war was Reginald Leonard Phillips. He was born on 22 April 1922 to Leonard David Phillips, who was an engineer and an air-raid warden during the war, and Gertrude Maria Phillips, who was a housewife and worked in a munitions factory during the war.

At the time Reginald joined up, the family were living at 5/14 Heath Green Road in Winson Green. He was working as a builder. Reginald came from a family who were no strangers to military life. His Uncle Fred had fought and died in the Great War. Reginald decided to join the forces with his friends before the war started.

He joined the Royal Army Service Corps and trained at the Territorial Drill Hall, Golden Hillock Road, Small Heath, in

Reginald Phillips in uniform. Courtesy of David Phillips.

1938–1939, and his role in the war was as an artificer, becoming a lance corporal. Artificers are those skilled and experienced in working in mechanics. He also trained and worked in Birmingham, Drayton Manor Park, Blunder Sands, Liverpool – where he experienced the eight-day Blitz – and he was also present at the D-Day landings in Normandy, France, in 1944.

He did have leave during the war, finding himself back at home, but instead of resting he was involved in the Birmingham Blitz too. He witnessed the blowing up of the BSA factory and his parents' house was also damaged.

He was demobilised in 1946 but became one of the job casualties. His building job had

Reginald's regiment. Courtesy of David Phillips.

Mr Reg Phillips with his regiment, enjoying some downtime. Courtesy of David Phillips.

Reginald's unit having some down-time. Courtesy of David Phillips.

Enjoying the water. Courtesy of David Phillips.

gone so he joined the engineering factory where his dad worked – Hunt-Mitton Ltd. His Uncle Fred had also worked there before he fought in the Great War.

Reginald revisited his old training drill hall in Birmingham forty-seven years after he'd last been there. He lived into his seventies and lived and died at home in Chorley, near Bridgnorth. He rarely spoke about some aspects of his war experience.

The women were not ones to shy away from war-work, and even Bournville works had female employees who joined the forces. As reported in the September 1940 issue of the *Bournville Works Magazine*, they had over sixty female workers in the forces. Many

Reginald standing outside the former drill hall. Courtesy of David Phillips.

women became nurses or First Aiders during the war – some of them having very little experience or training. They also worked under the Civil Nursing Reserve Scheme at local hospitals. It was not an easy job with the main complaint from these workers being that their legs and feet 'ached like billy-ho'.

One of these women was Miss Mildred Murray, who was working at Hollymoor in the X-Ray department and enjoying it. She commented: 'I certainly see a great deal at which to marvel.'

Miss Mary Caswell also enjoyed her work at both Dudley Road Hospital and in the Emergency Hospital. At the time of the report in the *Bournville Works Magazine*, she said that they hadn't got any patients in and the 'only occupants

Miss Mary Caswell. Courtesy of Cadbury Archives and Mondelez International.

of the beds are hot water bottles'. That was soon to change with the Blitz. In the infirmary she noted that most of the patients there were suffering from chronic illnesses, being 'old and helpless'. She found bath times particularly arduous work.

Another trio of nurses, Joyce Hartland, who was an employee in the transport office, Lilian Jones and Connie Shenton, who both worked in the gift office, now worked at the General Hospital. Although all three ladies enjoyed their new challenge, they often said how they missed working at Bournville. Jenny, who worked on a male surgical ward missed the evening tennis sessions at Bournville, the walks in the grounds and chatting at lunchtime.

Lilian, also on a men's surgical ward, was surprised by the fast-pace of the work:

> It is just like the Christmas rush every day. As fast as we get rid of one patient (cured, of course), we seem to have two more.

Despite the challenging work and tired feet, she was still in good spirits:

I wonder if those socks I knitted in my set of comforts are not up to standard, and all these corns are a judgement on me?

Connie worked on a women's surgical ward where, as part of her many duties, she was expected to prepare the breakfasts, alongside the orange and lemon drinks and then lunch. 'If I start telling you about the patients, I shall find myself writing a book!' she said.

Another nurse at Hollymoor, Greeta Nichols, who worked previously in the wages office at Bournville was also happy in her new role:

I am quite sure that anyone taking up nursing with any enthusiasm will feel more than repaid for all the labour extended.

She found one area of her work fascinating. 'One of the most interesting things about it is the opportunity it affords for studying one's fellow men!' She also commented at having to leave her

Greeta Nichols, pictured centrally, amongst the convalescing male patients at Hollymoor. Courtesy of Cadbury Archives and Mondelez International.

bed regularly at 3am when there had been fighting in France and convoys of injured men had to be received and treated. Something she thought 'not calculated to make Hitler any more popular'.

She painted a picture about what it was like when the men arrived in the ward:

> *And then they would come. Rows and rows of dirty, unkempt, tired men, sadly in need of ministrations. But what a transformation we worked on them! Bowls of water, clean clothes, and a meal make men out of wrecks – and they did so very much appreciate the first sleep.*

But it wasn't just nursing the women were involved in. Two women serving together in the Women's Transport Service (FANY) were Kathleen Harmer, from the wages office, and Myra Wilson, who worked in the cost office. They drove ambulances and said that even the two-ton Austin vehicle was not difficult to drive.

There are, of course, many more men and women from Birmingham who joined the forces and various other organisations, but there are far too many to mention here. Without their work and dedication, however, the war could have been a very different experience for those left at home.

CHAPTER SIXTEEN

The End of the War

The end of the war couldn't have come quickly enough for the people of Birmingham. Six years of hardship and a lot of the city reduced to rubble had taken its toll. When the news came that Hitler had committed suicide in his bunker on 30 April 1945, which led to the surrender of Germany, Victory in Europe Day was a bank holiday on 8 May 1945.

This date was swiftly followed by the surrender of Japan on 15 August 1945. However, the Japanese administration did not actually sign their surrender until 2 September 1945.

Although there were many joyous celebrations that the six hard years of war were over, there was still much to be concerned about. Many thousands of servicemen were still abroad, awaiting demobilisation, which was to be staged – some not to return for several months after war ended. There was also the question of rebuilding and finding homes for those who had been bombed out in the city, and homes for the servicemen coming home.

The hopes of rebuilding quickly were doubtful. Alderman Bernard Alderson, who was chairman of the city's Estates Committee, couldn't see many houses being built for quite some time. This was because he was not convinced that there had been enough thought and organisation in the area. He thought that the main issue preventing the building of houses tied in with that of the sluggish demobilisation problem, which was preventing servicemen with the potential skills and experience from coming home and easing manpower problems in the industry. Until that happened, the city and many areas like it were in a quandary.

Celebrating VE day in St Owen's Road, Birmingham. Courtesy of Eileen Housman.

Bournville Works celebrating VJ Day, 1945, at Rowheath – Caption reads VJ plus 1 Day. Courtesy of Cadbury Archives and Mondelez International.

The children's VJ plus 1 day tea party at Bournville School. Courtesy of Cadbury Archives and Mondelez International.

To illustrate the extent of the housing crisis at the end of the war in Birmingham, Alderman Alderson pointed out that they received, weekly, in excess of 1,500 people calling at the department, alongside many more letters. He said that the lord mayor received hundreds of letters too for housing, when the truth of the matter was they had none to give. Alderman Alderson was sympathetic to their cause, calling the housing crisis 'pathetic, as it has an intensely human side'. He was worried for those servicemen yet to come home and the prospects of them securing accommodation too.

The department and the lord mayor had taken the important step to talk to the newly appointed Minister of Health in an attempt to get him to look into why demobilisation was taking so long and whether men with the skills and experience necessary for house-building could be released quickly. House-building was a priority but wouldn't happen without men and resources. Before the war came, the building trade employed 1.2 million men. Now, it was a mere 400,000.

The men waiting to come home had risked their lives for their city and country. They had given up home comforts and precious time with their families in order to secure victory. They were coming home, but not to the heroes' welcome of housing and jobs. Many of them, as many civilians, would find themselves homeless and unemployed. The council were not impressed at how the servicemen were being treated. Birmingham people took care of their own, but the building crisis prevented that.

The city's register of servicemen stood at 20,000. But that was just the tip of the iceberg. There was another ordinary register of civilians desperate for housing to be considered too. Because of the sheer numbers involved, the council had no choice but to engage a points system to allocate the meagre amount of housing that was available. Their plan was, in the interim, to build 4,500 prefabricated bungalows that would be temporary (some are still standing today), but there was frustration at the slowness of the construction, with the council only having keys for forty of them.

As well as building prefabs, the council were also converting 600 empty houses into 1,200 flatlets. Five hundred further homes had been requisitioned and void houses had been served with notices.

Another thing that was a big issue at the time was that of workers who had stepped into the servicemen's shoes and taken on their jobs, temporarily. What was to become of them when the men returned? The men had been promised jobs when they came back, but was that feasible?

There was a piece in the 1 September 1945 issue of the *Birmingham Mail* highlighting how the worker in Birmingham could 'laugh at his misfortune'. They were talking about the number of redundancies that would be made at various factories, trades and businesses across the city now that war was over. The issue even ended up with a little song written about the workers' predicament, which was sung to the tune of *John Brown's Body*. One of the lines was to the point:

> *For the bonus has diminished, and the wage is sure to drop,*
> *and another list (redundancy) is coming very soon.*

It wasn't just the building trade concerned about the slowness of demobilisation. The fire brigade also sent their frustrations to the paper. There was a claim that of a total force of 1,200 firemen in the city's area fire service, 700 ex-Auxiliary Fire Service men had requested demobilisation but had had their applications declined.

The writer of the letter had been in the fire service since the outbreak of war and thought the service was currently running a 'chaotic system'. There was no room for manoeuvre when it came to losing more men. They complained that, unlike the police force, who had a date to work to when they could be released, the fire service had to wait for more recruits to join before they could leave. There was also the question of what kind of service the new recruits and those who stayed behind would be coming into. Was it to stay under the control of local authorities or be nationalised?

He also highlighted that it had taken 1,000 men to protect the city against fire, but before the war 310 men had done so sufficiently. The *Birmingham Mail* was sympathetic to both parties and, in order to give a more balanced view, told readers that people still had to do their civic duties when it came to fire protection, regardless of whether the war was over or not. They disputed the statistics the writer had produced. It was the Birmingham City Fire Brigade he was talking about when he stated 310 men, whereas the 1,000 men total was to do with Area 24 coverage, which included not only Birmingham but Coventry, Nuneaton, Sutton Coldfield and Atherstone too – a considerably larger zone than Birmingham alone. They also operated on a twenty-four-hour-on/twenty-four-hour-off shift system, which although it suited the men would need more of them to succeed.

With demobilisation came the issue of resettling servicemen. A talk was given by J.C.S.M. Hutchinson, who was the regional appointments officer of the Ministry of Labour and National Service, to the Birmingham Rotarians. He was concerned with those servicemen who had no experience or qualifications in industry or commerce, but who had gained rank in the forces through their 'courage, leadership and initiative'. He wanted to tap into this skill-base of both men and women of 'higher appointment standard', who missed out on the relevant training and experience because they accepted war service.

When it came to rebuilding parts of the city that had been damaged in the air-raids, these skills were a tremendous advantage to the process and local community. He called upon the Rotarians to help with the process of advising people of the training available. Specially trained personnel would interview the servicemen and women with those leaders in business and industry telling the department what vacancies they had.

The *Birmingham Mail* had its own opinion on demobilisation. Along with the rest of the country, it had been listening closely to the broadcast given by the prime minister about the government's plans. They said they were initially pleased that he had pledged to have 1 million men demobilised by the end of that year (1945), but once they had thought about and discussed it, they realised that the Bevin Plan would deliver far from what was expected. It was to manage the redistribution of the workforce, like a sticking plaster on a deep gash.

The *Birmingham Mail* was keen to point out that there were 5 million skilled and experienced men still in uniform, still abroad doing nothing of any worth, who were needed back home to start rebuilding Britain's towns and cities damaged by the Blitz, as well as providing the extra homes for those coming back. They thought the government hadn't done enough.

They were concerned that the 'chaos' that had followed the Great War would not happen again. The process of demobilisation was just too slow and would do little to ease the labour crisis. The feeling was that Britain could not move forward again at a productive and efficient speed until more men had been demobilised. It wasn't just the building trade that was struggling. Those businesses and trades involved in export and stocking the country's shelves were also experiencing difficulties. They were warning of 'empty grates' for the coming winter with the fuel crisis biting too. The war might have been over, but it was still a case of all-hands-on-deck and make-do-and-mend.

With the end of the war came a sense of optimism that the menfolk would be back soon. It had been a difficult war for many women in Birmingham who had been left to fend for themselves and their families. For many, tragically, their men were never to return, and even those who did were changed due to the horrors they had witnessed and endured whilst fighting abroad.

For many others, though, while the talk in the news was about the surrender of Japan and Singapore, it meant that their men were coming home and many women in the city were featured in the pages of the *Birmingham Mail* having received such news.

Major T. Christopher RA of the Regular Indian Army had sent a telegram to his fiancée, Alison Dowler, that although he had been a prisoner-of-war in Singapore from 1942 he was expecting to be home soon.

Similarly, Mrs Kate Cox of Lozells Street had heard that her husband A.B. Cox, a Royal Navy Reservist, had been set free but was waiting for transport to bring him home. He had been in Hong Kong when he was captured in 1941. His son was serving in Burma and he hadn't yet seen his only grandson.

Thoughts were also turned towards how the city would commemorate its fallen. There was already the Hall of Memory, which was opened in 1925. It was built to help commemorate the

12,320 people from the city who died in the Great War, and a further 35,000 who were injured.

The foundation stone for this building was laid on 12 June 1923, by the Prince of Wales, and was opened by H.R.H. Prince Arthur of Connaught on 4 July 1925. The money raised to build the hall came from charitable donations and cost £60,000 (£6,096,000). It was built by local people.

There are four bronze figures around the building that represent the army, navy, air force and women's services and were designed by Albert Toft. He was born in Handsworth into a family renowned for their pottery and sculptures, himself an apprentice to Wedgwood from where he moved on to sculptures, including nudes and war memorials. He also designed monuments, one of which being the Edward VII statue in Birmingham.

The area around the Hall of Memory has changed several times over the years, but when it was built there was a colonnade

The Hall of Memory. Author's Own.

The Hall of Memory showing two of the four bronze figures. Author's own.

where the Birmingham Repertory Theatre is now situated. The hall and colonnade were designed by S.N. Cooke and W. Norman Twist and constructed by John Barnsley and Sons and John Bowen and Sons. When Centenary Square was built, the colonnade was moved to the site of the old St Thomas's Church in Bath Row as part of a peace garden.

The interior houses the rolls of honour for both the First and Second World War fallen. There is also a third roll of honour that has the names of those servicemen and women who have lost their lives in war and campaigns since the Second World War.

In 1995, on the fiftieth anniversary of VE Day, due to the campaign headed by Marjorie Ashby, the peace garden became the home of a new plaque that was to commemorate those who had perished in the Birmingham Blitz. But Marjorie and her campaigners, including Dr Carl Chinn (later to become Professor)

Roll of honour inside the Hall of Memory. Author's own.

felt this did not do those who had died justice, and in December 2000, a remembrance service was held in St Martin's Church. Eventually, this saw the formation of Birmingham Air-Raids Remembrance Association (BARRA). They were eventually able, through various charitable donations, to have the memorial situated in Edgbaston Street, but had to secure planning permission. Funds were also kept, enabling BARRA to keep the people of Birmingham and further afield informed on what they were about and what the memorial meant. It was unveiled on 8 October 2005. Once it had been unveiled, BARRA found seventy-six other names had to be added.

There is a monument in the Bull Ring commemorating the civilians who lost their lives in Birmingham's Blitz called the *Tree of Life*, designed by Lorenzo Quinn. He was born in 1966 and a lot of his work is inspired by human hands. During the war there were 365 air-raid alerts with seventy-seven being real. From 8 August 1940 to 23 April 1943, Birmingham suffered a severe battering, which resulted in 9,000 people being injured, with 2,241 of these losing their lives. The Halcyon Gallery donated the monument to the City of Birmingham in association with BARRA and Birmingham City Council.

There was also a monument erected by the Bournville and Cadbury workers themselves to honour their fallen.

Birmingham covers a vast area and there are countless other memorials in the area, too many to include here, but it is comforting for those with family who remember the Blitz, or who had family who lost their lives, to know that, thanks to the work of BARRA, the council and others like them, they will never be forgotten.

Birmingham played an immense part in the war effort, both by those of its families who went abroad to fight and those who stayed at home to secure the streets and work on the Home Front. Housewives, children, single men and women – everybody did what they could, above and beyond, to help Great Britain win the war. They may have been battle- and Blitz-scarred, but they never gave up. It is their legacy that Birmingham is such a vibrant and industrial hub of business, commerce and culture today.

The Tree of Life. *Courtesy of BARRA/Jacqui Fielding.*

The Tree of Life. *Courtesy of BARRA/Jacqui Fielding.*

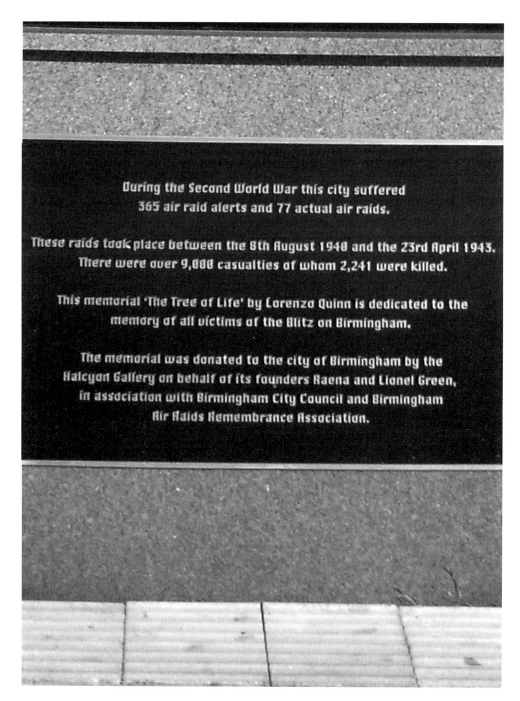

The Tree of Life. *Courtesy of BARRA/Jacqui Fielding.*

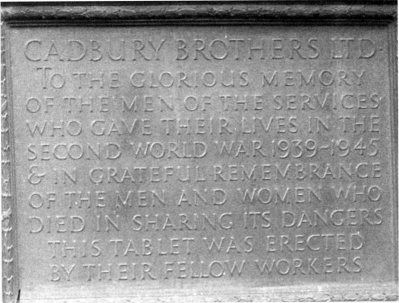

The monument at Bournville. Images taken by the author, reproduced with permission of Cadbury Archives/Mondelez International.

Index

Prisoner-of-War, 119
Pritchett MC, T.B., 46
Proficiency and Skills at Arms
    Badge, 50
Propaganda, 94, 112, 119
Prudhoe-on-Tyne, 96

Quakers, 20, 97–8, 102
Quarry Lane, 118
Queen's College Chambers, 87
Quincey, de Victor, 27, 28
Quincey, Jeanne, 28
Quincey, May, 27
Quincey, Raymond, 28
Quincey, Victor, 27, 29
Quinn, Lorenzo, 187
Quinney, A., 93
Quinton, 144

Rabone Hall, 131
Radbourne Road, 114
Radford, Captain F.F., 49
RAF, 24, 26, 29–30, 33–35, 47,
    104, 141, 149–50, 165
RAF Fighter Command, 35
Rajah, HMS, 28
Randall, Joan, 60
Ration books, 77, 80, 83, 121
Rationing, 21, 58, 63, 65, 72,
    76–7, 79–82, 86, 88, 90, 94,
    108, 110, 135, 138–9, 165
Rawll, Major R.H., 48
Rea, River, 1
Recession, 11
Red Cross, 112
Red Cross Fund, 126
Rednal, 118

Regional Appointments
    Officer, 182
Regional Chief Constables, 37
Regional Food Officer, 83
Regular Indian Army, 183
Relief stations, 123
Reserved occupation, 17
Reservoir, 7, 50, 53, 69
Rhineland, 12
Richards, Sergeant A., 53
Ridgeway, Mr, 117–18
Rigby, Jean, 61–2
Robinson, Mr, 114
Robinson, Olive, 88
Roll of Honour, 186
Rollason, Mr, 30
Rollason, Mrs, 30
Rollaston Wire Company, 40
Romans, 1
Rose and Crown Hotel, 126
Rose, Stoker, 121
Rotton Park Street, 50
Rover, 26
Rowe, Sergeant G.H., 52–3
Rowheath, 33, 89, 107, 179
Rowntree, 100
Rowton House, 65
Royal Army Medical Corps
    (RAMC), 105, 111–12
Royal Army Ordnance Corps
    (RAOC), 105, 117
Royal Army Service Corps
    (RASC), 104–105, 116,
    148, 169
Royal Artillery, 38, 116, 148
Royal Birmingham Society of
    Artists, 88